PRAISE FOR *THERE I WUZ!*

"When we come across an aviator wit[...] off the page. Eric Auxier is such an a[...]
—Karlene Petitt, Airline Pilot; [...] Correspondent, Author, *Flight For Safety*; and *Flight For Control*

"With his signature brand of riveting prose, Captain Auxier brings aviation to life in vivid, spellbinding color."—Tawni Waters, author, *Beauty of the Broken*

"Like watching a slide show of the life of a pilot. You will seriously enjoy this fast-paced read."—PaxView Jeff (paxview.wordpress.com)

"Great stories from the pointy end of the plane. Extremely entertaining, enlightening, and just plain funny."—Stall Recovery (flymaine.blogspot.com)

"Eric takes our minds on a wild ride of fun, laughter, and hair-raising flying tales. A thriller in every sense of the term!"
—Jean Denis Marcellin, pilot, author, *The Pilot Factor*

PRAISE FOR *THE LAST BUSH PILOTS*
"TOP 100, NEW NOVELS, 2013"—Amazon.com
"You won't want to put it down while the midnight sun still shines!"
—*Airways* **Magazine**

"Eric Auxier is the next Tom Clancy of aviation."
—Tawni Waters, *Beauty of the Broken; Siren Song; Top Travel Writers 2010*

"I flew through *The Last Bush Pilots* in one sitting, keeping my seatbelt securely fastened. A fast-paced tale, thoroughly enjoyed."

—John Wegg, Editor *Airways* Magazine

"The author paints pictures with words that are every bit as beautiful and moving as anything ever drawn or photographed."—Aviationguy.com

"A page-turning adventure novel, where surviving is only half the battle."
—Mark L. Berry, airline pilot-author, *13,760 Feet*

"As an Alaskan bush pilot, reading *The Last Bush Pilots* was like a glance in a mirror."—CloudDancer, *CloudDancer's Alaskan Chronicles.*

"Mark Twain published the ultimate adventure known as *Tom Sawyer*. Jump ahead 100 years to *The Last Bush Pilots*. There is risk, danger, love, and yes there is death. This is the last frontier."—PaxView Jeff (paxview.wordpress.com)

PRAISE FOR **CODE NAME: DODGER**
WINNER—Remington Literary's Search for a Best First YA Novel

"An all-time fun ride! The author hit a big win on this. Looking forward to the series!"—Karlene Petitt, author, *Flight for Safety; and Flight for Control*

"Like *Harry Potter*, this YA novel is fun for kids of all ages. While ostensibly a spy thriller, full of twists and turns, high tech spy gadgets, ruses and deceptions, *Code Name: Dodger* goes far deeper, into conflicted characters, their complex relationships, and the true meaning of love, loyalty and family."

—Tawni Waters, *Beauty of the Broken; Siren Song; Top Travel Writers of 2010*

ALSO BY ERIC AUXIER

The Last Bush Pilots
Code Name: Dodger
ADVENTURES OF CAP'N AUX
(capnaux.com)

GOT EBOOK?
If you purchased this book via Amazon, get the e-version for only $1.99!
Extra stories! Color photos! Videos! Hot links!

Link: goo.gl/FX9n3E

THERE I WUZ!

ADVENTURES FROM 3 DECADES IN THE SKY

VOLUME I

BY ERIC "CAP'N AUX" AUXIER

Published by EALiterary Press.

Printed in the United States of America.

ISBN-13: 978-1499127515
ISBN-10: 1499127510

For such permissions, contact the author at capnaux@gmail.com

THERE I WUZ!

ADVENTURES FROM 3 DECADES IN THE SKY

VOLUME I

TABLE OF CONTENTS

DEDICATION

Dedicated to the memory of William Brian Rock
07/18/1947-04/26/2014

Thank you for taking care of my big sister all these years.
Your incredible devotion to your family reminds me of my own father.
Thank you for the great memories, and for my awesome nephews.
You will be sorely missed, my brother.

FORWARD by Karlene Petitt

International Airline Pilot, Author, CNN guest correspondent

Karlene straps on her Boeing 747

While there are many amazing things about being an airline pilot, among the greatest are the adventures we live through in pursuit of our passion. The old adage, "What doesn't kill us makes us stronger" should actually be: "What doesn't kill us makes us wiser."

With this wisdom comes a pilot's need to share their stories with those little birds that follow in our contrails. We take them under our wings to guide them. Often our lessons are nothing more than examples of what not to do. But these stories always entertain with laughter in tow. When we come across an aviator with a gift for story telling, those adventures jump off the page. More than that, the words grab and pull you into the excitement and you become part of the story.

Eric Auxier is such an author, and *There I Wuz* is the book.

Whether you are an airline pilot or student, an aviation fanatic or passenger, there is something for everyone. Eric's adventures will take you around the world, from Alaska to Thailand—and you'll even find yourself soaring through the Grand Canyon. You will dance with clouds, watch the sky fall, and spar with hurricanes. But above all else, you will smile. Laugh aloud. And, many times, you'll find your mouth hanging open in awe.

Welcome aboard the journey of a lifetime—Cap'n Aux's life.

Buckle up—you're about to takeoff.

Karlene Petitt is an International Airline Pilot type-rated in the B744, B747, B757 B767, B737, B727 and the A330. She has spent 21-years of her airline career training pilots. She is the author of two best-selling novels, **Flight for Safety** *and* **Flight for Control***, and is a frequent guest aviation expert on CNN.*

Karlene holds an MBA and MHS, and is currently enrolled in ERAU's PhD program. A mother of three daughters and grandmother of seven, Karlene lives in Seattle, Washington with her husband.

Visit her excellent blog over at KarlenePetitt.com.

PREFACE—Welcome Aboard!

Ayy! The Cap'n Hard at work

Ask any pilot how they started flying, and you will hear a love story. One much like mine.

From age five, I dreamed of a life in the cockpit. But what dream worth pursuing is not rife with pitfalls, dangers and challenges? Otherwise, the world would be filled with cowboys, ballerinas and astronauts.

While the aviation career isn't for everybody, it always makes for a good tale. Life is an adventure, and life in the sky, exponentially so. However, as an industry, we seem to be moving toward a future dominated more by automation and less by fundamental flying skills. Looking back, I feel especially blessed to have lived in a historical sweet spot—somewhere between *too dangerous* and *too boring*—where survival by one's seat-of-the-pants and stick-and-rudder skills were more important than programming a flight computer, where *flying* the plane trumped *managing* the plane. Just as the characters in my novel, ***The Last Bush Pilots***, we seem to be nearing the end of an era of freedom and adventure in the sky. We are becoming the bear cubs orphaned and caged by the inexorable march of bureaucratic red tape we call Progress.

But, as seasoned Chief Pilot Dusty Tucker says to *cheechacko* (greenhorn) bush pilot DC in the novel, "The adventure's still out there, son. You just gotta go find it."

Well, found it, I have—in spades! From the first moment my feet left *terra firma* in a hang glider as a daring (make that foolish) teen, to my head-first dive into the wilds of the Alaska bush, from my extreme adventures in the Caribbean fighting off hurricanes to finally landing in the left seat of a major airline, I feel blessed to have lived more adventures than most. It's both kept me young, and aged me beyond belief.

Many of the stories in this compilation can be found in one form or another on my blog at capnaux.com, NYCAviation.com or other publications such as *Airways* Magazine, *Plane & Pilot*, *AOPA Pilot* and the like, but have never been presented in one body of work. In addition, you will find articles never before published, stories behind the stories, and even several guest posts by fellow pilot-authors. Except where noted, every story in this work is true, and represents what is, for me, a literal lifetime of adventures in the sky.

The book is loosely arranged by theme; read it cover to cover, or jump around to whatever tale strikes your fancy.

Whether you are a seasoned warrior of the sky, fledgeling pilot about to embark on your own lifetime of adventures, or a "chairborne" avgeek, I invite you to sit back, relax (well, as best you can, some of these stories are pretty hairy) and enjoy the ride!

Eric Auxier, April 6, 2014
Phoenix, Arizona USA

SECTION 1: Inflight Emergency

You're the Captain: Explosive Decompression!

Originally published by NYCAviation.com

"BOOM! In back, you hear screams. Then silence."

'Scuze the obvious pun, but . . .

Let's start this book off with a bang, shall we?

Written just days after the mysterious disappearance of Malaysia Airlines Flight 370 (at press time it is still missing), NYCA asked me to do a piece about a possible explosive decompression which, early on, was one of the leading scenarios.

While this is one of the few fiction pieces in this book, for any airline pilot, it very well could be real.

You're the Captain of Fantastic Airlines Flight, 123. You're an hour into your flight from Paris to Tokyo, cruising over the Baltic Sea at 40,000 feet.

You've assigned PF (Pilot Flying) duties to your trusty FO (First Officer) Mark, who is flying the plane on autopilot. As PNF (Pilot Not Flying) on this leg, you work the radios and run support. In the two cockpit jumpseats behind you sit your IROs (International Relief Officers,) who are just about to take over for the middle part of the 11-hour flight while you and Mark go to the back and rest up for landing. You reach for the Flight Attendant call button. But suddenly . . .

BOOM! Explosive decompression!

For the next ten seconds, the cockpit becomes a hurricane, with papers and small loose objects flying. The windows frost over. Suddenly, the temperature plummets to minus a jillion. You, Mark and the two IROs all frantically snatch and don your full face oxygen masks. No time for checklists; at 40,000 feet, you have a mere 15-20 seconds of useful consciousness.

With a hiss, the mask sucks snugly around your head. Fumbling in the blind (the oxygen mask is also fogged over) you select 100%, forced flow. You peel away the thin plastic anti-fog lining and suddenly you can see again.

"I have the aircraft!" you shout.

"You have the aircraft!" your FO, previously the pilot flying, acknowledges. You reach to kick off the autopilot—and realize it has already disengaged itself. Grabbing the yoke, you ease the nose over into a high dive while simultaneously cutting the engine power to idle. You need to get down ASAP, but you dare not increase speed: the aircraft has no doubt suffered structural damage. She's still alive and flying, and you want to keep her that way.

"Ding Ding! A dozen alarms all clamor for your attention."

She's sluggish, her right wing shuddering and trying to drop, the tail yawing hard to the right. You kick in left rudder and hold left aileron just to keep her going straight. The hurricane is gone, but there's still a cacophony of sound assaulting your ears. *DING! DING! DING!* goes the Master Warning, flashing red and competing with a dozen amber emergency procedures suddenly popping up on your ECAM (Electronic Centralized Aircraft Monitor), all clamoring for your attention.

The FO silences the Master Caution. "Mayday, mayday," he yells out on the radio, his shouts muffled by the microphone in his O2 mask. "Fantastic Flight 123, declaring an emergency. Explosive decompression, executing a rapid descent. Turning off course to heading 360."

In back, you hear screams and someone making a PA announcement. You can't make out the words, but you know it's a flight attendant bleating out instructions and imploring everyone to stay calm, while shouting in a frantic, panicked voice herself. Then the screams and PA suddenly go silent. They've either donned their own masks, automatically deployed by the pressure loss —or they've all passed out. There is one more noise though: that of rushing air. Somewhere back there, you have a gaping hole in your machine. But you already knew that.

The altimeter blazes through 32,000', spinning backwards in a blur like a mad scientist's time travel clock. Your vertical speed, normally 1-2,000 feet per minute up or down, is now passing through 8,000 fpm. You're over water for the moment, so you're aiming for an altitude of 10,000'.

"Call the back," you order. "We need to know what's going on."

"Already did, Cap'n," your trusty FO replies. "No response."

Not surprising. They're probably all out cold. Just in case, you toggle the PA switch. "This is the Captain," you say, in the most calm, commanding voice you can muster. "Remain seated. The situation is under control." That's all you have time to say.

Right now, you're a tad busy working on that little bit about, "the situation is under control."

"Explosive decompression Checklist," you order. It's a backup for what you've already done, but you need Mark to read it, just in case you've missed something. And in the "fog of war," even the best-trained pilot can easily miss something. Again, Mark has already anticipated your next command, and has the QRH (Quick Reference Handbook) out and ready to read. You've got your hands full flying the plane, so he reads and does it aloud.

"'O2 Masks—Deploy' he quotes. Deployed. 'Cabin masks—Deploy' Deployed . . . Turn off the airway and descend to MEA (Minimum Enroute Altitude) as soon as possible. Do not exceed speed at time of failure. Assess damage and adjust flight path and controls accordingly. Land at nearest suitable airport.' Explosive Decompression Checklist complete!"

"The altimeter spins backwards in a blur, like a mad scientist's time travel clock."

"Roger that," you reply. "MEA's below 10,000, so that's where we're headed for now." The airspeed begins to increase. You gingerly pitch up to bleed it off. A glance at the altimeter: 25,000 feet. You're low enough now to ease in some speed brakes. Instantly, the plane begins to shudder violently. No good. You ease the brakes back off. It's then you notice: the right engine's out—and on fire.

"ECAM actions," you bark. Mark reads the top checklist that's popped up on your screen.

"Engine Number Two, failure and fire, Skipper."

"Understood," you reply.

Mark begins reading and doing the on-screen emergency checklists. "'Engine two thrust lever—idle' idle. Engine two master switch—off,' confirm?" he asks. His hand is poised to pull the number two kill switch, but again in the fog of war, the last thing you want to do is shut down the wrong engine.

You hazard a glance at the Master switches and see he's got the proper one. "Confirmed," you reply.

"Off! 'Engine Two Fire Bottle—Discharge'" There is a brief pause, before Mark announces, "The fire's out, Captain," with an obvious sound of relief in his voice.

"Roger that, continue with ECAM actions."

You glance behind at the IROs. Strapped in and masks on, they look back at you.

You have an idea. While Mark has his hands full securing the plane with oodles of checklists, you've got two fully qualified pilots at your disposal sitting right there.

"Kathy," you call to the first relief pilot, "I need you to get back there and see what's going on. Don the PBE (Portable Breathing Equipment) and take the crash axe. If they're all out, put masks on our gals up front and try to revive them. And if you see any structural damage, get back here and report it ASAP!"

"Aye aye, Cap'n!" comes her smart response.

"Charlie," you call out to the second pilot, "get up here and find us the nearest suitable pavement."

"Yes, sir!" Charlie springs out of the jumpseat, kneels by the pedestal, and punches data into your flight computer.

"Captain," the FO chimes in.

"Yeah, Mark?" you reply. "ATC advises Stockholm's 170 miles ahead, about 10° right of course. Denmark's behind us 250 miles."

Damn. You missed that radio call. The fog of war again. You contemplate the situation. Denmark's behind you, and nearly twice as far, while requiring twice as much maneuvering. And you still don't know what's going on with the plane.

"Stockholm sound good to you, Mark?"

"Affirm, Captain," he replies.

"Charlie?"

"Agreed, sir."

"OK, looks like we'll be partying with the Swedish Bikini Team tonight," you say, hoping the joke will relieve a little of the tension. "Tell ATC that we want vectors for Stockholm Arlanda."

As Pilot in Command of an emergency aircraft, the world is at your beck and call. You don't ask, you tell. You read the altimeter. Blasting through 16,000 feet. You ease back on the stick, coaxing the plane out of its earthly plummet, aiming for 10,000 feet level off. You pull the mask off.

"Captain," Kathy chimes in, back from the cabin. "Everyone's knocked out back there. No injuries that I can see. Flight attendants are groggy but coming to."

"Damage report?" you ask.

Kathy takes a big breath. "The second, aircraft-right, overwing exit is gone. It looks like it ripped into the upper right wing and took out a few spoilers in the process. Thank God the overwing slides didn't deploy. Yet."

"Roger that," you reply. "Fire?"

"No flames from number two engine, just smoke now. It's just out there windmilling, so it looks like you gents got 'er shut down properly."

"OK good. You two to get back there and help the flight attendants check all passengers out. They should be coming to soon. Double check for any injuries and all seat belts locked tight. If anyone is freaking out over the missing door nearby, try to reseat them."

"Aye aye," they reply.

"This is the Captain. Brace for impact."

The next half hour goes by in a blur. The checklists have all been run, and the cabin has been secured for an emergency landing. On touchdown, you'll have only one thrust reverser. However the landing gear has mercifully deployed, with all brake systems reporting green. You have elected to land on Stockholm Arlanda's Runway 01L. At nearly 11,000 feet, it's the airport's longest. You've also chosen not to deploy the flaps due to the structural damage, so you'll be coming in mighty hot.

As the air gets thicker, you notice that the aircraft is becoming difficult to control. Your left leg is throbbing from fighting the rudder all the way down. Through gentle yoke movements and a lot of hard rudder, you're finally lined up on final approach. The runway looms ever closer in the windshield. At 500 feet above the ground, you toggle the PA.

"This is the Captain. Brace for impact."

"Over the fence, on target, sink 800," Mark announces. You pull the yoke up slightly and the airplane flares.

The plane slams onto the runway, but you knew it would. There is no time for finesse under the circumstances. At least she's on the ground in one piece. Well, two pieces. You left a door somewhere back there in the Baltic Sea.

You press the toe brakes and throw number one into full reverse, fighting the sudden left yaw. The plane shudders and screams. And then, finally, mercifully, it stops. You set the parking brake and toggle the PA one last time.

"This is the Captain. Remain seated. The situation is under control."

The cabin erupts in cheers. You take a deep breath, your heart pounding. Suddenly you notice about 200 TV trucks and cameras behind the airport fence, broadcasting you on live feed around the world. Book deals, endless talk shows and somewhat unwanted fame is in your near future. But for now, you're just thankful to be alive.

Photo courtesy of Mark Lawrence at amateuravphoto.blogspot.com

Everyone wants to hail you as a hero. Even your own flight crew now wants to pat you on the back. You shrug, and say something you'll be repeating on TV talk shows for years to come:

"I was only doing what I was trained to do."

Grand Crisis Over Grand Canyon

Originally published in AOPA Pilot Magazine as Trickledown

Cessna 210 formation flight over "The Ditch"

Let's take a trip in the Way Back machine here, and enjoy one of the first stories I ever published in a magazine. Over the years, I've learned that the easiest stories to sell are the ones that involve an inflight screw-up of some kind. Hmm, no wonder I've been able to become so "well published" . . .

"I don't like my engine doing strange things while flying over God's most utterly nonrunwaylike terrain."

The inflight emergency. It's something you train for, but when it happens, your brain turns the consistency of 50-weight. That's how I felt the day it happened to me. I'm still shaking the sludge from my ears.

I had been flying a Cessna 210 (single engine, six seat prop plane) for a Phoenix-based charter company. The plane was older than my pilot's license, so annoying little failures of a gauge or radio was almost routine. Perhaps that explained my lack of alarm when the cylinder head temperature began reading abnormally cool during a sightseeing flight over the Grand Canyon. I was too busy playing tour guide to worry about another mischievous instrument. But just in case, I closed the cowl flaps and continued through the Canyon.

After a few minutes I glanced back at the instruments. The cylinder head was dropping even lower, but what really caught my eye was the low oil temperature. Either both instruments were failing simultaneously or the engine was running cold. Cold was better than hot, especially on an Arizona Spring day, but it puzzled me.

An eerie feeling crept like a centipede up the back of my neck. I don't know about other pilots, but I for one don't like my engine doing strange, inexplicable things while flying over God's most utterly nonrunwaylike terrain.

But the engine purred on, as serene as the calm before the storm.

I breathed a sigh of relief as we passed the last of the Canyon's sheer cliffs and turned south for home. We were now flying over desert—desolate, but at least relatively flat; no mountains to swat us down if the engine decided to take a vacation.

"I knew each passenger was mentally screaming, 'My God! We're gonna die!' Hell, I was."

I glanced back at the gauges: needles below the scale. This engine was running on ice cubes. Then the fuel gauges dropped to zero. Now this whacky engine was running on air! I'd had enough of this.

"Uh, folks," I muttered, "the engine seems to be running a bit cool, so we're going to make a *precautionary* landing at Williams airport to examine the situation."

I'd flown passengers long enough to know not to use loaded words like *emergency* landing, or instrument *failure*. But the passengers sensed the truth, for as I was speaking, my voice faded—the intercom died. I pulled off my headset and repeated the comment, shouting above the din of the prop. I waited for one of them to scream, *"My God! We're gonna die!"*, but they all smiled gallantly back, looking only slightly uneasy. But I knew that each was mentally screaming that phrase. Hell, I was.

The problem with a small airplane is that there's no wall separating you, the pilot, from the passengers. They are all essentially in the cockpit with you. They see your mistakes, your hesitation, the sweat drip from your troubled brow. And they see the instruments fail.

"What's that?" the passenger in the copilot's seat asked, pointing to the DME (Distance Measuring Equipment.) Instead of reading groundspeed and distance, it flashed *ERROR! . . . ERROR!*

"Oh, that's nothing." I replied unconvincingly, and quickly shut the damned thing off.

I called Williams unicom. No response; the radios had failed.

Approaching downwind, I lowered the landing gear switch.

Nothing.

The gear was stuck, sound asleep in the gear well.

I cycled the gear handle up and down. I pulled the gear circuit breaker out and in. I switched the battery master off and on. I did everything but jump out and pull the damned wheels down by hand.

It must have been like a sauna in that cockpit, as sweat poured from me like fuel from a sump drain. I turned and slowly surveyed the passengers. Still all smiles. I simpered back and returned to my dilemma.

"The Landing gear was stuck, sound asleep in the gear well."

I forced myself to think . . .

Why would everything fail at once?

The battery!

Through the fog of war, it finally dawned on me: the alternator must have failed, and the battery automatically took over. With all radios and lights on, the power had drained in minutes. At least the engine, powered by self-driven magnetos, was in no danger of stopping.

But that didn't help the landing gear.

I switched all radios and lights off to conserve any last trickle of battery juice and reached for the emergency manual gear extender. On the Cessna 210, this comes in the form of a pump, located on the floor between the two front seats. I pumped the handle madly, pushing and pulling the lever like a water pump, all the while flashing that nervous and utterly unconvincing, *just routine, folks!* smile.

I was just about to pledge 50% of my future income to the Lord when the last remnant of battery power came to my rescue: the green *"gear down and locked"* light blinked cheerily on. The flaps swallowed the rest of the battery juice, but we landed without further incident.

I learned several lessons from that fiasco. First, scan the instruments often. As it turned out, the alternator failure had been intermittent, and the scant few times I glanced at the gauges, the ammeter had shown no discharge. Had I been more attentive, I could have diagnosed the problem at the outset.

Second, when the battery supplies the only power, it dies—and *fast*. If you're flying IFR (in clouds) or at night, it's critical to shut off all nonessential equipment immediately.

Finally, don't rush through any emergency that isn't immediately threatening. *Use the checklist*. With an engine fire, the pilot must react quickly and by memory to secure the blaze and land. But with a landing gear failure, the pilot has time to read methodically through each item on the checklist, or have a passenger call it out to him.

Having not used the checklist, I forgot to pull the gear circuit breaker. If I'd accidentally left the gear handle up, the battery could have tried to raise the gear right at touch down!

Also, the *Alternator-Out* checklist calls for a flaps-up landing. If I had to abort the landing and climb out, the battery might not have been strong enough to raise the flaps, perhaps leaving me to wallow into the trees.

Pilots should practice regularly the memory items required in a crisis. But for all other problems, use the checklist.

For when the emergency comes, the rational, thinking mind goes.

SECTION 2: Lessons Learned (the Hard Way)

I Nearly Wet My Pants

Originally published as a Blogging in Formation story

This is the first of several *Blogging in Formation* stories to appear in these pages. Each month, our team of eight pilots blog about a given subject. For the first few days of the calendar, Avgeeks feast on our cornucopia of aeronautical tales. Karlene Petitt, Mark L. Berry and Brent Owens, whose words grace these pages, are three of our team. You will find our *BIF* links on my capnaux.com site. Check it out!

The subject of this *BIF* story is called, perhaps a tad euphemistically, *My Best Instructional Moments . . . .*

"Brrrrrrrooowwww" went the sound of my engine winding down.

I nearly wet my pants.

Why? Minor detail: I was still 10 miles from the airport, at an altitude of 3,500' in a single engine Grumman Cheetah.

I was a 20-something flight student working on a college degree and a CPL (commercial pilot's License.) My college, Cochise, had a runway right on campus. A "poor man's Embry Riddle," I liked to call it.

Located smack in the heart of nowhere and six miles north of the Arizona/Mexico border, the campus offered wide open, clear blue skies for us fledgelings to spread our wings. While the Sonoran desert below offered relatively flat terrain, none of us newly-hatched chicks wanted to brave the cactus-strewn, rattlesnake- and scorpion-infested wastelands in a 4-seat accidental glider.

And yet, *There I Wuz . . .*

But more on that lesson later.

Speaking of nearly wetting my pants . . .

On one of my most memorable cross country flights at the same college, I found myself an hour away from my destination—Deer Valley Airport, in the northwest Phoenix Valley—when I had to go pee.

Really, really bad.

Checking the fuel supply, I firewalled the throttle. The engine screamed. The airspeed indicator leapt from 115 kts to . . . 116. I asked Albuquerque Center for a direct routing to destination. No such luck. I seriously considered diverting to an emergency alternate. But try explaining that to the dean.

> *"My bladder's overpressure relief valve was so far past its design limit, I was near panic."*

Inch by maddening inch, I inched toward my destination. After an eternity, the Phoenix Valley loomed into sight. Deer Valley lay on the opposite side of the metro area—another 10 minutes to cross.

Having received my PPL (Private Pilot License) training in the Valley of the Sun, I was more than familiar with the old landmarks. However, my bladder's overpressure relief valve was so far past its design limit, I was near panic. As I frantically scanned the city, nothing looked familiar. Fortunately, Phoenix ATC vectored me straight to Deer Valley airport, where, after several bladder-jarring bounces, I touched down. I fast-taxied to the parking area, set the brake, killed the ignition and eased out of the cockpit. No "hopping out" for me; any fast movements, and my jeans would be a darker shade of blue.

I waddled to the bathroom, doing my best to look nonchalant.

Today, I am happy to say, all my flights are on airliners with plenty of lavs available. But I think, even after 17,000 more hours under my belt since that fateful day, my internal overpressure relief valve has been fully trained to come nowhere near its design limit ever again.

Our Lesson Here:

—Always take a whiz before flight.

—Don't load up too much on coffee.

—No lav aboard? Carry your own: an empty, gallon-sized water jug.

(Not gonna comment on what the female equivalent of this might be.)

My first "Command": a Cessna 210

As for my engine winding down?

My heart leapt in my throat. I immediately lowered the nose to keep airspeed. My brain switched into overdrive, calculating the probabilities of deadsticking in to our runway, and searching for an alternate, snake- and cactus-infested gully in which to land.

Just like the problem of diverting to take a whiz, I knew the best outcome would be that I'd earn the constant ribbing of my peers, and some horrid nickname that I'd never live down.

At worst, I'd die.

"At worst, I'd die."

That reminds me of another good lesson, that of James Richards (not his real name), my fellow Alaska bush pilot in Juneau. One day, while taxiing his Cessna 207 around a line of airplanes, he took the turn a little too hot and tight. His wing dinged another wing. Result: two busted nav lights. No big deal. But it earned him an "incident" in the FAA playbook, and the dubious nickname of "Crash."

He hated that name with a passion, but it stuck with him for the rest of the season. Today, "Crash" Richards is a senior Captain at Alaska Airlines.

Captain Richards is also the original inspiration for the name of my character Jake "Crash" Whitakker, the legendary bush pilot in *The Last Bush Pilots*. Larger than life, Jake is equally adept at landing planes and ladies— and "crashin' 'em," too.

Our Lesson Here:
—Always take it careful and easy around airplanes; at worse, you'll die; at best, you'll earn a reputation and nickname you don't want.

"The crisis lasted a microsecond, but taught me a lifelong lesson."

So, about that engine failure . . .

I immediately reached down between the seats and switched fuel tanks. The engine sputtered back to life.

I landed without further incident, but with my heart still racing.

That's it. The crisis had lasted only a microsecond, but it taught me a lifelong lesson.

You see, the Cheetah was equipped with two wing fuel tanks, and a pilot has to switch between them to maintain an even burn. Being used to Cessnas that had only one tank—or, that is, two wing tanks that automatically drained equally, no tank switching necessary—I was naturally not used to such fuel monitoring. And I had drained one tank dry.

But after that day, I never failed to maintain a completely even fuel burn.

Our Lesson here:
—Always monitor your fuel load, even when you know you have plenty.

Teaching is a License to Learn - by Mark L. Berry

Airline Captain-Author-Blogger-Managing Editor for Airways Magazine

The Cap'ns at rest: power lunch with Mark on a layover.

Our first guest essay is by Mark L. Berry. Mark is one of my favorite authors, and is a member of our *Blogging in Formation* team.

This piece was originally published in *AOPA Flight Training* magazine in the February, 2011 issue. It is also Chapter 12 in Mark's gripping memoir, ***13,760 Feet—My Personal Hole in the Sky*** (available in paperback and Kindle formats on Amazon.com.) A pilot for the very airline that claimed his fiancée on TWA 800, Mark's ***13,760 Feet*** chronicles his excruciating psychological odyssey as he claws his way back to inner peace. Dovetailed with this is the wild story of his flying career, which regales the reader with a bird's eye view—warts and all—of the gritty, often comical, reality of airline life.

Mark is also the author of two novels and numerous companion songs that accompany his writings.

Check out all of his works at marklberry.com.

Teaching is a License to Learn

*Note: the companion song, "*Teaching is a License to Learn*" is performed by, and co-written with, Simon Ashby:
Link: marklberry.com/memoir/teaching-is-a-license-to-learn/*

As a seventeen-year-old primary flight student, I was still making the transition from the hijinks of high school to the seriousness of college. Mary, a petite lady in her early twenties with shoulder-length light brown hair, was my Embry-Riddle flight instructor for the course from post-solo through my private pilot's license. As she prepared me for this next level of aviation responsibility—a license that would allow me to fly without supervision and even grant me the authority to carry my own passengers, though not for hire —she rapidly grew tired of telling me that my hand belonged on the throttle from takeoff through a thousand feet to keep the power from sliding back.

We'd discussed this in the cockpit before—over the wide variety of noises that makes conversation challenging. The cockpit is right behind the four-cylinder engine, much like in a car. But mounted to that engine is a six-foot spinning propeller that we look through while we fly. Sitting behind the prop wash adds a vaguely lawnmower sound to the engine noise. Next, the only significant ventilation in a Cessna 172 is provided through outside air scoops. Drive at twice the highway speed limit and then open a couple of side windows about a quarter of the way down for a similar effect. And Florida is hot, so leaving the vents closed is not a practical option. To defend against this onslaught of sound, we roll up small, cylindrical foam plugs and let them expand inside our ears. Then we make sure to face each other while speaking, and we shout. With the effort it takes for an instructor to impart wisdom during flight, Mary did not enjoy repeating herself.

Shortly after rotation in a Cessna 172, when I used both hands to pull back on the yoke, she asked, "Where does your hand belong?"

"Right here at the end of my arm."

This was not the response she was looking for. It earned me a lecture about treating her with respect, taking my training seriously, and on and on and on. The foam earplugs did nothing to defend me against this emotionally delivered lesson. It didn't help that my flight partner in the back seat couldn't stop laughing. I eventually had to admit she was right, but I remember feeling at the time that her reprimand was overdone in both length and volume.

Two years later I was sitting on the other side of that four-seat, one-hundred-and-sixty shaft-horsepower trainer and it was my turn to instruct. I'd made it through commercial, multi-engine, instrument, and certified flight instructor courses. I was assigned to teach advanced instrument training and commercial maneuvers. Many of my students would fly with me one day, and then fly solo for a day or two to practice what I'd taught them.

My students and I sit side-by-side
Sometimes it's a turbulent ride
Sometimes new ones get terrified
That's when I have to stay dignified

I was at my desk—one of eighty identical metal versions spread around an open, circular instructor room—giving a last minute briefing to Jim and John before our flight, when up walked our head mechanic with a look of fury in his eyes. He slammed down an aircraft clipboard that served as its logbook, which rang with all the subtlety of metal on metal. He had both my students' and my attention. "Look what your smart-aleck student wrote in my clipboard!" He used his thumb to implicate Jim while looking at me, and then continued, "Here, I'll show it to you."

Keeping a cool personality
It's harder than it appears to be
While flight instructing daily
Teaching is a license to learn

The mechanic picked up the clipboard, opened it, and then handed it to me. Having released some of his anger in the act of slamming my desk, he read out loud from memory what I could see was an entry from the day before, "Autopilot lands hard and the number three laser ring gyro is out of tolerance." Jim and I looked at each other, but the mechanic continued, "He may think it's funny making up stories, but writing up a hard landing in my logbook, even as a joke, requires me to do an airframe and gear inspection. The logbook isn't a coloring book, and our aircraft aren't toys. If he can't get that through his thick head, he can learn to fly somewhere else."

I waited to see if he was done. It looked like he'd continue if I didn't intervene, so I said, "Jim, what do you say to the man?" I hated making him feel like a child, but it seemed necessary to acknowledge the mechanic's point. I didn't just want him to go away, I wanted him to go away happy that he'd been heard loud and clear.

"I'm sorry, sir."

The mechanic opened his mouth to speak again so I cut him off, "Well, I hope that just about covers the proper way to fill out a logbook. Lesson learned, don't you think?"

The mechanic said, "Don't let it happen again," and turned to leave. He reached three paces away and then turned and came back. I worried he had more venting to do. Instead he reached down and grabbed the aircraft clipboard from me, turned to leave again, and did his best storming-away impersonation. I had worked with him before and this was uncharacteristic of his nature. The logbook write-up must have really pressed a nerve.

Every mistake that a student can do
Is a chance for me to learn too

Jim looked like a defeated man, and he seemed as if he expected me to add another chewing out to his day, right before we needed to go out and fly. Not much learning was going to happen that way, so instead I asked, "What's a laser ring gyro?"

The bad cop had left. Since I have a hands-across-the-throttles relationship with my students in the small Cessna cockpit, I was more than happy to accept my role as the good cop. It hadn't been so long ago that I was getting myself into trouble for inappropriate comments, though mine were verbal and Jim's written. Plus, I couldn't stop wondering what a laser ring gyro was. In addition to being a tension breaker, my question was a sincere request for information.

Keeping students from crashing me
Giving advice and acting naturally
While flight instructing daily
Teaching is a license to learn

I never asked what advanced aviation magazines Jim was reading, or if he had a parent in the airline industry. I just knew that I still had a lot more to learn. My job was to find the best way to teach my students and keep my eyes and ears open for information that they were also able to teach me. I learned lessons that day on how to manage upset people, how to balance the stick and the carrot as learning tools, and I even picked up some advanced technical knowledge. And, I was getting paid for the experience.

And just an FYI, so you don't have to deface a logbook to find out— laser ring gyros are internal components with no moving mechanical parts that provide the guidance for inertial reference systems. Basically, they allow an airplane to know where it is without any outside navigation signal from the ground or a satellite. Cessna 172s obviously don't have them, at least not university trainers. But that didn't prevent me from learning about them while teaching in one.

I show students the proper procedures
How to handle the throttles and mixtures
How to plan for unexpected encounters
And how to emergency land into pastures
Keeping students from crashing me
Giving advice and acting naturally
While flight instructing daily
Teaching is a license to learn

Again, don't forget to check out the companion song, "Teaching is a License to Learn" performed by, and co-written with, Simon Ashby: Check it out at: <u>marklberry.com/memoir/teaching-is-a-license-to-learn/</u>

For more funny logbook write-ups, check out the story, "Zen and the Art of Aircraft Maintenance," in Section 6.

Go Jump off a Cliff!

A previously unpublished story

A child's First Solo: age 17! With Instructor John P.—now a SWA Cap'n

"Only my instincts flew; my brain took a vacation."

Introduction: At the age of 17 I flew solo in a Cessna 152. As any pilot knows, the experience is magical and life-changing. You can ask the oldest, grizzled, cranky retired airline captain about his first solo, and he will immediately grow misty-eyed, look off into the distance, and mumble garbled poetry about life, love, and adventure. In his mind, he has instantly transported back to that golden moment, decades earlier, when he first tasted the magic of flight.

I too share this wondrous experience. I have shared it several times on my blog as well, in a post entitled, "Judgement Day Hath Come!"

But what is not known is that, while I truly did solo a Cessna at age 17, that was not my first ship to solo. Indeed, at age 15, I flew a hang glider. I can not begin to describe the magic of that first flight, other than to say it changed my life. I had experienced heaven, and would never be the same for it. Never.

"Judgement Day Hath Come" was written after I flew that hang glider—not the Cessna. I only later adapted it to the story of my first Cessna solo, and is every bit an equally valid story in that context.

While the Cessna solo achieved an important milestone in my life, it cannot match the intense adrenaline rush of that first kite ride.

Go Jump Off A Cliff!

"It was a gently sloping hill. To me, it was Mount Everest."

I had waited ever since I could remember for this day, yet now that it had arrived, fear nearly paralyzed me. Now I stood—literally—within grasp of my ultimate dream. I had never once thought of the danger involved with hang gliding. And in a frustrated world of broken dreams, I began to feel I was what that world called this sport—crazy. The sense of adventure that lives instinctively in a 15-year-old had grown, expanding to build a pressure inside me. A pressure that could only be released once I jumped off that mountain. Actually, it was merely a gently sloping hill; to me, it was Mount Everest.

Perhaps it was the brave fool inside a young teen, oblivious to the concept of death, that persuaded me to volunteer for the first flight. The older students in the hang gliding class wasted no time arguing. I guess the whole concept of the hero is to tackle one's fears at full charge and destroy them. But I wasn't doing this for the glory, I was doing it for me. To free the shackles that life sets upon us from birth, and few escape.

One thing hang gliding teaches you is patience. It seemed like forever, waiting for the perfect wind for takeoff, all the while fear churning my stomach, anxiety gnawing me with butterflies. The wind finally settled, as I secretly hoped it wouldn't, daring me to take off. I had no choice.

Now or never.

With trembling hands, chattering teeth and that damn pressure bursting out at every pore, I strapped in. I felt the cold aluminum of the trapeze bar across my back as I lifted the hang glider. The sails ruffled in the breeze as guy wires clinked at their joints. The instructor steadied the support wires in front of me, looking for my ready signal.

Ready, hell! I could barely move! It was all I could to breathe.

I gave a quick nod. And ran.

"My God, what am I doing? I hope there is life after death!"

It's a funny feeling that comes to you as you know you're committed to something, like diving off the high board into freezing water or walking onto stage on cue, a thousand people watching. Everything seems to slow down, giving you more time to wallow in thought. It's sort of a morbid feeling of foolishness, like waking up and saying, "My God, what am I doing? How stupid could I be?" Followed quickly by, "Too late. I hope there is life after death!"

That's what I felt as I sprinted for takeoff. My brain overloaded in a confused mass of emotion—and short-curcuited. The instant my foot left the ground my mind went blank. The universe sailed silently by in slow motion. Only my instincts flew the kite; my brain took a vacation. Euphoria, pure and divine chased away my fear.

I wanted to scream out, but I was too busy with torrents of emotion. That's all it was, emotion, and not a material thought pressed through. My mind was truly blank, a feeling unequalized by anything, anywhere. Not even in dreams.

I spent the entire day jumping off that mountain.

It seems a paradox that something so blissful could only be obtained by first drowning in fear and terror. As the Steve Miller song goes, "You've got to go through hell before you get to heaven."

Fearless: age 15!

25

"I spent the entire day jumping off that mountain."

Ask the newest solo student or the most stoic airline captain what flying is like: he will immediately grows a wistful smile, looks off to the sunset with gleaming eyes and starts reciting garbled poetry about freedom, beauty and life. You've heard the song a thousand times and can't understand. That is because it is truly indescribable. It has to be experienced. And hang gliding is the closest we will ever get to being a bird.

I didn't realize until I was 18, about three years after that first, miraculous flight, how profound a change it had made in me. Before, I was a grouch, a spoiled brat who rebelled against my parents because I was frustrated and confused. Since then, I became patient, objective, mature. It was amazing; a complete 180 degree turn from pessimism to optimism.

I had become Jonathan Livingston Seagull, living not only on the earth but above it.

Inflight Undercover Sting Op! - by Brent Owens
Professional Pilot-Author-Blogger

Along with Karlene Petitt and Mark L. Berry, Brent Owens is one of our *Blogging in Formation* team.

A professional pilot and writer, Brent brings his considerable general aviation flying experience to the table. He is the creator of iFLYblog.com and fixedwingbuddha.com, and has written for several online and print aviation publications. And if you're an aircraft owner, Brent's ebook, *The Pilot's Guide to Flying on a Budget* will save you tons of cash!

As an avid general aviation enthusiast, Brent can be found flying his Van's RV-8 around Central Ohio or just hanging out at the local airport with friends.

In this adventure, Brent fancies himself an undercover Drug Enforcement Agency pilot . . . until the plane decides to run its own "undercover sting" operation!

"Cool! I'm like a drug interdiction pilot!"

(Author's note: no specific dates, locations, or names are used in this story to protect me from any bad guys that were on the receiving end of this operation.)

As a starving flight instructor working my tail off to make ends meet, occasionally I did some uh, shall we say, "interesting" flying.

One flight that stands out is a trip to a nearby big city and back. Normal ops, except this was a dual-purpose mission. One of my students was a local deputy on loan to the DEA as an undercover agent. As a result, some of our lessons were done with "alternative plans" in mind.

In this case, we needed to do a cross-country flight for his license, so he coordinated going to this particular location to pick up some . . . *items* . . . from the DEA office for a little sting operation.

Cool! I'm like a drug interdiction pilot!

Brent and I trade high-fives while passing thru KPHX.

We flew up, and it was a beautiful clear day, but hot. We shut down and loaded the "items" on board and jumped back in. We were only on the ground fifteen minutes. But it was just long enough to heat-soak the engine compartment. An older model Cessna 172 with a 145 hp Continental engine, it was not exactly over-powered.

We'd flown into one of the smaller downtown airparks, but no problem for a light airplane. Buried in the middle of suburbia, however, an engine failure would not turn out well.

"We were hovering 200' over the buildings and running out of ideas."

My student was flying from the left seat. We lined up to depart southbound. The takeoff was sluggish, but not too unusual on a hot day for this airplane. Then, at about 200' above the ground, we stopped climbing! The throttle and mixture were full forward, airspeed at best climb, nose in the proper pitch attitude . . . but the vertical speed was zero.

"I have the controls," I announced.

Of course, the airplane doesn't care who's flying, so the situation didn't improve. We were hovering over the expanse of houses and buildings at 200' and running out of ideas. Declaring an emergency, I made a tear drop turn back to the runway with the throttle firewalled.

But turning caused us to sink.

Thank the angels, we had just enough altitude to clear the hangars and land downwind. We touched down just a few hundred feet from the end of the runway. With the brakes locked, we went off the end into the grass. Fortunately, it was only a few yards past.

Although the rollout was rough, the airplane came out unscathed. A few yards further and we would have crashed into an embankment—and then a creek.

(Disclaimer: Turning back to a runway with an engine failure at 200' will almost certainly never work. Remember, we still had some power being produced.)

We looked that 172 over top-to-bottom, and couldn't find anything wrong with it.

"With the brakes locked, we ran off the end of the runway."

Was I imagining things? Did I do something wrong? Did my student do something wrong, and I didn't catch it?

It's hard not to be introspective when you narrowly avert an accident that no one can explain.

Then my dad—one of the company's mechanics—made the discovery. The carburetor filter was clogged with red lint! It had restricted the fuel flow, especially in a climb on a hot day.

But where did the lint come from? Using a flash light and mirror, my dad ripped the fuel system apart and discovered what was left of a red shop rag left inside the fuel tank! Over the years, the rag had slowly decayed and ended up clogging the filter.

Yep, that rag had run its own undercover sting op—and nearly "busted" us!

Oh, and speaking of which, my passenger-student-undercover agent did bust his own bad guys!

Visit Brent at iflyblog.com and fixedwingbuddha.com

Save oodles of dough by reading his book, "The Pilot's Guide to Flying on a Budget"

fixedwingbuddha.com/pilots-guide-to-flying-on-a-budget/

SECTION 3: North to Alaska

My Favorite photo from Alaska. On final into PJNU, summer, '88

The Sky Fell

Published in Airways *Magazine May, 2014*

This story, recently published in *Airways* Magazine, is the true story of a watershed moment in my bush flying career—and my life. A fictional version of it serves as the crux of the story for DC in ***The Last Bush Pilots***.

Just like the novel itself, this piece is dedicated to my wonderful friend Steve Wilson, lost to us in the bush in 2007. Steve leaves behind a legacy of Alaska aviators, as his children now fly in the Southeast.

Dedicated to the memory of my good friend Steve Wilson, career Alaska bush pilot.

The sky fell. There's no other way to describe it. The sky just . . . fell.

My fellow Alaska bush pilots had explained it to me once. At the time I had only half-believed them. Surely they were spinning yarns, telling tall tales. Ghost stories over Chinook beers at the Red Dog Saloon in downtown Juneau, to spook the gullible Alaska *cheechacko* (greenhorn.)

But *There I wuz*, ripe old age of 25, with a "whopping" 2,200 flight hours driving a single engine, 6-passenger Cessna 207 prop plane laden with Tlingit Indian locals, freight and fish through the perpetually soggy skies of Southeastern Alaska, when it happened.

Born, raised and flight trained in the "severe clear" sunny skies of Arizona, this wet world was as alien to me as Planet Pandora. I might as well have been beamed there to fly dragons.

"Dude, get up here now! They need pilots yesterday!" my buddy Kevin had exclaimed over the scratchy phone line only a few weeks earlier, calling from Planet Alaska. "I'm flying for a great charter company out of Juneau."

Staring out the window into yet another sunny, 100-degree day in Phoenix, my brain could not begin to fathom the perils of his offer. Having just lost my jobs and my "First Big Break" in a poker game (see my blog) I was desperate for employment. Moreover, I needed something exceptional to push me to the next rung on the aviation ladder. Something to make a prospective employer go, "Wow!" Something to bag me that Holy Grail of aviation, the Major Airline.

"I'm there," I replied, and hung up. This, I had decided in a microsecond, was the "Wow" I was looking for.

A boy and his plane: cruising the Juneau Icefield.

Alaska bush pilot: the most hazardous job in aviation. Scud running (flying visually, dodging low clouds, rain, fog and "cumulogranite"— mountains lurking inside clouds) to remote villages, fishing canneries and logging camps.

Between the utter lack of instrument nav systems and extreme mountainous terrain, there was no other way to get the job done.

I would either launch my career or die.

Hanging up the phone, the butterflies hit. Launch my career or die? What the F*&%$ did I just get myself into?

As a *cheechacko*, you had to quickly learn the gig: fly along the pine tree-walled shoreline; navigate by matching coast, mountains and landmarks to the VFR Sectional chart in your lap; cross ocean channels at high enough altitude to glide to shore, in case of engine failure. For that was your only hope: land on one of the scant few, bolder-strewn beaches or sand bars. Or crash into the carpet-thick forest, frigid ocean channel, or *cumulogranite*.

Your destination was always a short runway or dirt strip carved out of the forest or mountainside. Buzz the field to chase away the bears, moose and other varmints, circle back and land.

Oh yeah, and did I mention weather? In Alaska, it's all about weather. A 1-degree spread between temperature and dew point (the temp at which air turns to cloud) is a good day. A 1,000-foot overcast with three miles visibility in rain and fog, spectacular.

Despite lucking out and experiencing such "spectacular" conditions for my first few weeks in Alaska, the low overcast and fog constantly provoked claustrophobia. About "Pucker Factor 3," according to Kevin—referring to how tight one's sphincter got during the flight. On a scale of 1-10, of course.

And then comes the wettest month on Juneau's record . . .

"And then comes the wettest month on Juneau's record."

. . . Pressing down the coast of Admiralty Island from JNU (Juneau) to AFE (Kake, a Tlingit village) at 800 feet agl, I am steadily forced lower and slower by the slate grey overcast and fuzzy fog .

Whitecaps appear on the water; the wind's picked up. Light turbulence kicks in. My passengers and I bounce along as if driving down a dirt road.

Power back. Slow from 115 knots to 90. First notch of flaps out . . . 2nd notch. Pitch over and ease lower. 750 feet . . . 700 . . .

Pucker Factor doubles to 6.

Ocean spray; the wind's really whipping. Moderate turbulence. We're slammed against our seat belts. 4-wheelin' now.

Pucker Factor 8, Mr. Sulu.

Squinting through my Serengeti sunglasses, I can just make out the turn of the coastline a mere half mile ahead. Barely time to glance at the Sectional chart. At least by now I've memorized the route and terrain, which helps immensely.

But then it happens. The sky falls.

The rain turns to fog, which turns to cloud, which turns to rain, which turns to . . . Like a water balloon bursting, the black bottom disgorges from the cloud base.

Turning final to Kake—after buzzing the bears away.

600 . . . 500 . . . I push the yoke forward and dive, desperate to stay clear. My scant 1/2 mile visibility, myopic only seconds before, now seems a decadent luxury.

Dropping full flaps and slowing to 60 knots—the slowest I dare go—I yank and bank along the curving coastline. Treetops whiz by. No time for even a glance at the Sectional.

450 . . . 400 . . . the black forces me lower. I'm now level with the pines, blazing by to my right. A startled eagle takes flight from his nest—above me. A brown bear swipes at me yards below, his angry yellow eyes forever searing into my memory.

The engine screams. The landscape blurs. The turbulence pummels. My brain overloads with the maddening cacophony of sight, sense and sound.

So this is it. This is how I'm gonna go. And take a few innocent, trusting locals with me.

Launch my career or die—how stupid could I be? Stupid enough to kill myself and a few others, apparently.

"Pucker Factor 10:" I now know just exactly what that means.

Sweat trickles down my side. My eyes cloud over. Gripping white on the yoke, my hands shake. I begin to hyperventilate.

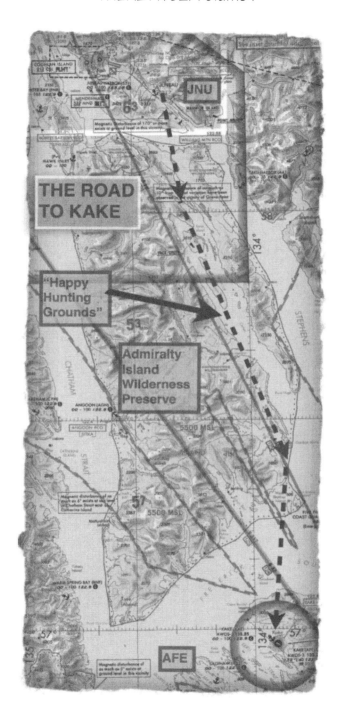

But then it happened . . .

The sky fell.

My family will be devastated, I think. Comfort each other with lines like, He died doing what he loved best. My fellow pilots would be equally devastated. But secretly think to themselves, I wouldn't have been that stupid. Silently thank the gods it wasn't them. This time.

"My family hunts down there."

The voice jars me. I shake my head, take a long moment to process its meaning. I chance a glance at the Tlingit passenger sitting next to me.

"Huh?" I manage.

He smiles back at me. "My family hunts down there," he says brightly, pointing down at the absurdly rugged terrain racing by in a green blur. "I got my first brown bear right . . . there!"

Is he frickin' kidding me? We're about to die, and he's sightseeing?!

Startled back to reality, I let out a nervous, confused chuckle, and bank slightly to let him see his "Happy Hunting Grounds."

That's when revelation hits. To this local, I realize, this is nothing. To him, this isn't a one-way flight to hell, it's a jaunt down memory lane. To him, Alaska is home.

Inexplicably, fear and panic evaporate. The shakes disappear. My breath slows to Yoga-calm. It's like Obi Wan Kenobi has whispered in my ear, "*Use The Force, Luke. Let go!*" And I do.

Elation washes over me as I realize: it's not a maddening cacophony, it's a beautiful symphony! And I see, hear, *feel* it all.

"So this is how I'm gonna go. And take a few locals with me."

I am a Jedi. Like my friend before me.

I deftly bank along sea and shore, earth and sky, dancing with Mother Nature to the symphony of water and air that She conducts.

And, all of a sudden, She relents.

At 300 feet above the ground, the sky stops. Reverses course. Turns from black to grey to white to . . . blue.

Climbing with the base, I see all the way across Frederick Sound to Kake.

With a knowing smile, She has lifted the veil, and for the first time, with new eyes—with *bush pilot* eyes—I gaze upon my beautiful mistress named Alaska.

And I know I am in madly, deeply, hopelessly, in love.

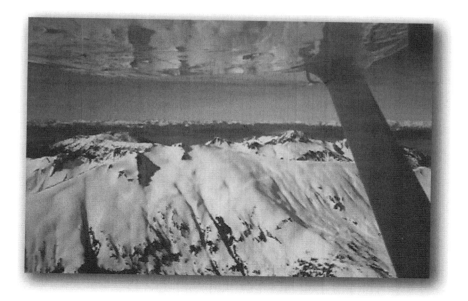

To this day, I wonder whether my passenger had made his statement out of complete innocence. After all, Alaska was as much a part of him as the black braids of his hair.

Or did he sense my panic and do his best to save me . . . to save us? I can certainly, unequivocally, say that he did.

Either way, I know it was Mother Nature herself who decided, "You know, *cheechacko*, I think I'll let you live. For now."

When I left Alaska after that brief summer to fly Twin Otters in the Virgin Islands, I left a big chunk of my heart behind.

And took with me a healthy new respect for Mother Nature.

Denali Mountain High - by Kevin Hufford
Career Alaska Bush Pilot

"I had just enough experience to be dangerous."

I am excited to include a special guest story by career Alaska bush pilot, Kevin Hufford.

People are always asking how much of my novel ***The Last Bush Pilots*** is fact and how much fiction. Mr. Hufford is the sole other person on the planet who knows the answer! Mr. Hufford is the original inspiration for the character of Allen, though he does *not* share Allen's personality. At the beginning of the book, main protagonist DC snags a job in the Alaska bush with a simple phone call from Allen. That exact situation happened to us: Kevin called me, and three days later I was on a plane for Juneau, Alaska! Our personal stories and the novel diverge from there.

I flew the Alaska bush for a single season; Kevin has flown there for decades. Needless to say, he has an encyclopedia full of wild, true tales under his hat. I asked him to pick one of his favorites to share with us.

"He was born in the summer of his 27th year, coming home to a place he'd never been before."
—John Denver, "Rocky Mountain High"

Kevin's bio, in his own words:

I was raised in the Arizona desert and came to love the wilderness. I was introduced to flying by my father. He bought a Cherokee 180 and took me for a ride. I was hooked. When I turned 27 it was time to combine my two passions and head for Alaska to look for a flying job.

I found a job at a hotel in Denali National Park as a maid, of all things. I had faith, and within a week I was teaching the heads of every department in the park how to fly. One of them owned a Cessna 150 but no license. So began my career as a bush pilot.

I'll never forget that summer. I remember hearing the John Denver song with the line, "He was born in the summer of his twenty seventh year, coming home to a place he'd never been before."

I could tell stories for hours but this one stays with me and is easy to write about. I have flown at 150ft and .5 miles vis in blowing snow over open water over 30ft waves with no land in sight at a 45 degree crab angle looking forward through my side window.

I did this stuff before GPS moving maps. What can I say? I get bored easily and need adventure. Never had the brains to pursue a proper living.

My kids have somehow turned out great in spite of me.

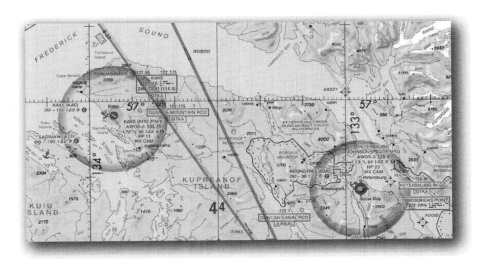

"I'd broken the Bush Pilot's Rule because, I thought, 'I was better'."

It was my third season flying in the Greatland (Alaska). I had just enough experience to be dangerous. I knew the basics and was supremely confident.

I was flying a Cessna 207 loaded down with frozen shrimp from the village of Kake to the town of Petersburg, on the opposite side of Kupreanof

Island. I chose to take the more direct route across the island, rather the longer one following the shore.

I entered Duncan Pass under a low overcast. I thought of the "rule of thumb" when flying through passes: Fly right at the bottom of the clouds and as far to one side as possible, maintaining sufficient room to turn around if needed. Never give up turning-around room unless you can see through the pass to the other side. I had broken this rule a few times before, and completed flights when others didn't because, I foolishly thought, "I was better."

I squeezed down in the middle of the valley's "vee," under the clouds and between the trees.

Suddenly, right in front of me, the clouds met the trees. I applied full power, pulled the nose up into the clouds and held my heading. I knew the mountains on both sides of me were steep and tall. I wondered if I would feel it if I hit one.

The only navigation equipment on board was a digital loran, which I tuned to Petersburg. After what seemed like an eternity, it finally picked up the signal. Petersburg was fifteen degrees to my left. I knew there was a ten degree left bend in the pass. I kept my current heading and climb while telling myself, "use the force, Luke!" to know when to turn to the loran heading.

I dialed up the company frequency and called my team mate John. I knew he was approaching Petersburg from the other side, so I asked for the weather conditions.

"100-foot indefinite ceiling," his voice crackled over the radio, "and one mile visibility at best. Take the long way around."

"Suddenly, right in front of me, the clouds met the trees."

"Uh, too late for that, I'm afraid," I answered, and switched to the airport frequency.

Still socked in the clouds, at about 2.5 miles out, I leveled off and made the turn. At 1.5 miles, I figured, I was nearing the end of the pass.

Taking a deep breath, I began descending.

At .5 miles and 500 feet, I knew, I was clear of the pass. 0.4 miles, 400 feet . . . 0.3 miles, 300 feet . . . 0.2 miles, 200feet . . . 0.1 miles, 100 feet . . .

I caught a glimpse of the runway under my right wing. I was at a treetop level downwind! It was pretty fuzzy, but I managed to circle around in a tight pattern and get on the ground.

I instructed the ground crew to unload the plane, and with wobbly legs, walked to the office for a much-needed cup of coffee.

That was the last time I ever made that mistake.

The Last Bush Pilots - Dusty Tucker

Excerpt from the novel, **The Last Bush Pilots**

One of the most revered characters in my novel ***The Last Bush Pilots*** is retired airline captain and SEAS' Chief Pilot Dusty Tucker. Yes, he is fictional, but he represents the persona and story of some of the last, great Alaskan bush pilots.

Born in Texas, raised in a P-51 over the German skies of WWII, Dusty is an aerial cowboy who trades a lucrative airline career for the rough and tumble and deadly Alaska bush. His story opens Chapter 4.

Chapter 4: Dusty Tucker

"He traded his cushy 90-passenger Electra for a taildragger."

Dusty Tucker was a veteran of the war—*The* War, as those of his generation called it. He'd served his country proudly, dueling Nazi Messerschmitts in the skies of Europe in that Cadillac of fighters, the P-51 Mustang.

Late to The War, the newly minted fighter pilot was shot down on his second mission. A French farmer hid him for eight months until Germany surrendered. In gratitude and lust, Dusty married the man's beautiful, starry-eyed daughter Suzette and whisked her away to his little lonesome hometown in the Lone Star State.

Upon arriving Stateside with his new war bride, he found his family's cattle ranch, the one he'd been groomed to take over, greatly diminished in size and stature. Moreover, oil was fast becoming the ranch's new herd, and Dusty found little interest in rounding up crude and roping wells. Dad had other sons to work the black stuff.

The world had changed, the States had changed. He had changed.

Commercial aviation boomed. Like hundreds of his fellow dogfighters, he jumped on board.

Whisking Suzette to the big city of Dallas, they enjoyed the pay and prestige of his new profession. Flying a DC-3, then later a Lockheed Electra, for Trans Lone Star Airways, he plied the skies across Texas and beyond.

Suzette made him a comfortable nest and bore him two daughters, Betty Lousianne and Bobbi Suzette—Betty Lou and Bobbi Sue for short. Nothing could be more perfect.

Nevertheless, Dusty found himself curiously restless. Despite the challenge of dodging seasonal thunderstorms, there was little adventure in the game for him. He felt like nothing more than a glorified bus driver. He no longer belonged. Where the hell he did belong remained a mystery. Through the boredom, something called to him, pulled at his inner conscience during the long, droning hours from Dallas to Denver and back. And then, one day, eighteen thousand feet over Del Rio, a single word popped into his head: Alaska.

"Dusty was his own weatherman, and what he saw out the window was the forecast"

His soul cried out.

"Dusty, you're crazy," Chief Pilot Baxter pleaded. "You're on the leading edge of your career. I'm telling you, this is the Roaring Fifties. Commercial jets are just around the corner. This industry will take off, and you'll be on top. You'll be an airline captain flying from Dallas to *London* nonstop. Think of that!"

He did—with distaste. Make more dough than God, but at what cost? Missing his kids' childhoods, that's what. The way he saw it, he had to choose between a life providing for his family and a life *with* his family. He gazed out the window at the drab countryside.

"To hell with it," he said to the cacti.

That spring, Dusty once again pulled up roots and whisked his wife, accustomed now to her lover's whisking, to Bethel, Alaska, 400 miles west of Anchorage.

To him, the tiny Yupik Eskimo village was home.

His family was shell shocked.

He traded his cushy 90-passenger Electra airliner for a Cessna. With the help of family oil stock, and a little cash squirreled away by the shrewd former airline captain, Dusty put a down payment on a brand new, 6-passenger, single-engine Cessna 185 taildragger, complete with optional ski package. Tucker Air Taxi was born.

Like most in Alaska, his was a one-man airline. He had no ticket agents, no flight attendants, no baggage handlers. Everything that went on board, he loaded. Inflight meals consisted of thermos coffee and a baloney sandwich.

"No maps or electronics guided him; his navaid was his eyes."

Through endless summer days and eternal winter nights, Dusty plied the vast skies between Eskimo villages, mining camps and trading posts. Up and down the Kuskokwim and Yukon Rivers he flew, between Aniak and McGrath, Galena and Fortuna Ledge, delivering mail, natives, trappers and prospectors, frozen fish and frozen government servants. Airfare depended on destination, client, and his disposition that day. Payment came sporadically, often in the form of gas, fish, or caribou steaks.

He eked out a modest living.

No satellites or TV forecasters beamed him the weather; Dusty was his own weatherman, and what he saw out the window was the forecast. There were often times that he took off into blue so pure it seemed sea and sky had traded places, that water and air were one friendly entity, only minutes later to conspire and force him down in a whiteout blizzard.

Few hangars existed to change a spark plug; Dusty was his own mechanic, and his garage was what he took with him. A survival kit always accompanied him as well, complete with food, blankets, medical supplies, and a Remington 12 Gauge shotgun. Little room was left for payload.

No gas stations existed enroute; Dusty was his own fueler. He learned where the local pilots stashed their emergency 55 gallon drums of avgas; which dirt strips, which patches of permafrost, which river banks. He stashed his own along his bread and butter routes, and never hesitated to tell the others about it. When weather forced him to circle above the Arctic tundra, he would land, siphon some juice into the Cessna's wing tank, then sit back, light a pipe, chat with a passenger if he had one, and wait for the pass to clear. On the next run upriver, he always landed and replaced what fuel he borrowed.

No maps or electronic gizmos guided him; his navaid was his eyes. For Dusty, "IFR" meant, "I Follow Rivers." Each bend in the stream, each mountain pass, each pool in the tundra he strove to memorize. His one extravagance was an ADF, Automatic Direction Finder, which pointed like a bird dog to any of the government's few low frequency radio navigation stations scattered across the land. But the beacons' low range, and fickleness in twilight or mountains, made their use somewhat limited. A far more practical use for the ADF, he found, was tuning into local village AM stations —more for companionship than navigation.

With skill, quick thinking and luck, the *cheechacko* survived by learning the hard way: on his own. Far from being the first, he was still one of the few, and therefore greatly appreciated.

Being treated like a big halibut in a small auger hole never went to his head. Dusty knew better. He gleaned tips and tricks from the other pilots. But the natives, so long used to living off the harsh land, taught him volumes. More than once, as Dusty pushed for a pass through the mountains, his Eskimo passenger would tap him and shake his head, then point to a landing spot. After several futile attempts, Dusty learned to trust their judgement nearly ahead of his own.

Even better, Dusty found, was what the pilots jokingly called the "Eskimo ADF." While looking for a microdot of a landing strip amidst miles of featureless tundra, he could take a furtive glance at his local passengers, whose gaze always stared, just like his ADF, at their destination. With a subtle change of course in that direction, he would nail the landing strip every time.

Every day taught him new lessons. Lessons, he found, that the fledgling Civil Aeronautics Bureau back in Washington never bothered to learn before slapping their rules willy-nilly upon the Alaskan skies. Far from Big Brother's arbitrary arm, Dusty and the other pilots simply chose to ignore much of them. Free to play by his own rules, Dusty had finally found his element.

He loved it. His wife tolerated it. His girls hated it.

For two years, the young women stoutly put up with cabin fever, six-month days and six-month nights, and frozen "honey buckets," the sarcastic euphemism for toilet pot. Finally, after a particularly brutal spell of 70-below wind chill, even Dusty's determination wore thin.

Sensing blood, the girls attacked.

"We're the only white kids in our grade at school," Betty Lousianne complained.

"So, it's a great chance to learn another culture," Dusty countered.

"We get teased and bullied every day," Bobbi Suzette added.

Dusty had no answer for that.

"How can we expect our girls to live in a tiny foreign village," Suzette asked in her seductive French accent, "where the sole excitement is betting on when the Kuskokwim River ice will break up?"

Bobbi Suzette began to cry. Betty Lousianne wrapped an arm around her and rocked. It had the desired effect.

Cocking his head sideways, Dusty looked at them. He turned his gaze out the window and into the darkness.

"Well, where would you have us live?" he asked.

"Anchorage!" they chorused.

Dusty held up his hands. "No way. Too big. Might as well have stayed in Dallas driving them fancy sky buses."

It took great reserve for all three not to scream out how much they wished he was back driving "them fancy sky buses." The three silently bit their lips.

With a resigned sigh, Dusty said, "To hell with it."

That spring, after breakup, the Tuckers moved from the Interior to the Southeast Panhandle, to Alaska's state capital, Juneau.

If You EVER do THAT Again! - by CloudDancer
Author, Airline Captain and former Alaska Bush Pilot

The Masked Crusader himself, with his trusty steed, the venerable De Havilland DhC-2 Beaver

"The end of the runway—and my life—is coming up all to quickly!"

I am equally excited to include another guest story by a personal friend of mine, a very experienced airline captain who goes by the pen name of CloudDancer

An arctic bush pilot for over twenty years, Cloudy is the author of four nonfiction books in a series called, *CloudDancer's Alaskan Chronicles* In a unique voice all his own (think, *Mark Twain meets Gomer Pyle,*) Cloudy writes about the wild, whacky and nearly always hysterical trials and tribulations he experienced while flying the Alaskan bush. Volume 3, however, is a brutally honest and serious book about, and dedicated to, those contemporary aviators of his whose lives were lost in the merciless Alaska bush.

Visit his homepage at: <u>clouddancer.org</u>

MORE FLAPS!
Excerpt from Chapter 3 of
CloudDancer's Alaskan Chronicles, Volume I

(Landlubbers note: Minimum flying speed in a Cessna 207 is around 63 mph—and much higher if overloaded. Normal takeoff flap setting is 10°. Anything beyond 10° is for landing only . . . at least, in the <u>normal</u> world!)

It was 60 miles above the arctic circle in Noatak, Alaska, population 246, in August of 1973. A 2800 foot gravel strip and I'm in the right seat of a (ahem) fully loaded 300 h.p. Cessna 207. I'm 19 years old, have about 280 hours, and this is my first "professional" flying job.

The left seat is occupied by my boss, Dan. He is the plane's owner and a real bush pilot, having flown these parts since he and his brother started stealing his uncle's airplane at age 12.

"Sitting in the five seats were . . eleven passengers."

Apparently either unable to count, or using some sort of "factoring equation" which escaped my notice in the study of 'rithmatic, Dan has loaded on a few too many passengers. Did I say a few? Sitting in the five seats behind me, there were . . I mean it—there were eleven people! I am NOT making this up!

Okay, so only five people were actually sitting in the seats. They each had someone sitting in their laps, and there was a little boy of about six or seven kneeling, wedged between the two front seats and the two second seats, basically wiping his runny nose on my left shirt sleeve.

Noting that they now have my undivided attention, I am assailed with a big chorus of, "Hi, pilot(s)!" from everybody, and two dozen questions all shouted at once, covering everything from my age, and marital status, to where I've come from and WHOSE my name again!

A very, very large man seated behind the pilot's chair, holding what has to be a 15 year old boy on his lap, sticks out a big right paw and introduces himself as Stanley, and his son Stanley, Jr. (I would come to learn that, like most native cultures, the eldest firstborn male child is almost always a "junior".)

I do note for the record as I look aft-ward from Stanley (Senior AND Junior) that the size of the passengers moderate the further aft you go; the one seat in the rear on the left being occupied by two kids small enough apparently that they don't have to be stacked up like a buncha' damn cordwood.

I snap my head to the right as Dan pops open the left hand door and jumps into the left seat effortlessly. Mouth still agape I watch him bang the door shut, clip his seat belt ends together, then shove the mixture forward while turning the ignition key. A quick glance out the front window confirms that the man is indeed starting the engine.

I practically scream at him, "Are you insane, man?" as the engines catches and settles down to an idle.

He says "Oh, don't worry. This is good! We make twice as much money on one trip and make twice as many people happy. See? That way everybody is happy."

The Legend unmasked: the early years!

"But.... but.... *Dan!*". I glance again over my shoulder to see if this was some sort of hallucination but ... no. All those people are still back there and indeed, they all seem to be very happy, laughing and jabbering away.

As Dan feeds in some throttle and the nose TRIES to come down on the nose strut a little, it dawns on me that I am apparently the only person out of all thirteen on this seven-place airplane who is just not happy.

It now registers on my wheezing and backfiring brain that, as Dan continues to feed in more throttle, the aircraft is not even moving—even though the brakes are off.

Finally, at about 2500 RPM, the plane "breaks away" and starts rolling forward. Our steady 85 % power setting continues to increase our taxi speed as I try to decide whether to bail out my door before we get going too fast.

But noting that Dan is whistling and seems quite comfortable (not to mention downright happy!), having briefly reviewed everything I know about aerodynamics—lift, thrust, weight, and drag (admittedly, not a whole lot at this point in my career)—like a moth drawn to the flame, I can't tear myself away.

The man doesn't seem *to be suicidal,* I think to myself, so, as we approach our turn onto this short, soft, warm, runway in our oversold and under-fueled Cessna 207, I decide to ride this one out. Will it be a "soft field" takeoff? Will it be a "short field" takeoff?

Finally I ask the 64 dollar question. "So . . . Dan. How's this gonna' work?"

"Oh?!" he says as though surprised I had to ask. His response to me? "USE MORE FLAPS!"

"Use. . . more . . . Flaps?????" I ask in bewilderment and Dan stops the airplane on the very slightest of upslopes leading to the beginning of the runway.

Although this was probably my last and only chance to escape this maniac and his sardine can with wings, I stayed for the explanation.

"Yes, I can see that the %$#@ing airplane is 'not quite ready to fly'!"

"Yeah. See . . . ," he sez, and then launches into the obvious (just not to me) explanation.

(My thoughts, as I listen to the unfolding, increasingly outrageous procedure are encapsulated in the parentheses . .)

"You see, we are a little heavy (good thing we didn't bring too much gas then) so we sure don't need any extra drag. That's why I haven't even put out our normal Flaps Ten yet. We'll start clean, see. And then, when we're about halfway down the runway, you put the flaps down to Ten when I tell ya' and I'll try to rotate her. But I'm almost positive she won't go at that point. (Yeah, I think I'd hafta' agree with that!)

"So, about three-quarters of the way down, I'll holler again, and you give me twenty degrees and we'll try 'er again. (Sa-a-ay what!?) 'N she might go, but most likely not quite. So, right before we get to the end—and wait 'til I say so!—You bang them flaps down to FULL, and when the gravel disappears under the nose I'll haul 'er off!!"

Okay I was wrong. The man is a freaking LUNATIC! Certifiable!

Unfortunately I hadn't noticed, being in sort of a state of semi-shock, that Dan had now shoved the throttle all the way in and we were creeping slowly up to the runway's edge as he kicked in rudder to line us up.

Wait!! Wait!! I can still jump!! We can't be going over twenty miles an hour!

A quick glance at the airspeed indicator (which is in MPH and starts at 40) confirms that indeed the needle still rests on the "dead" peg. Oh, too late. It's starting to quiver already with only about 10% of our 2800 foot relatively soft gravel runway already behind us. I look ahead and then back to the airspeed indicator as we bounce gently through the ruts and dips on our spring steel gear and am appalled to see it rising slowing through what I'm guessing would be the 20 MPH mark, if there was one.

And then Dan shouts out to me, leaning his head over toward me slightly so I can hear over the roar of the engine. "Now, see! We're starting off kinda' slow."

Ya' THINK? I say to myself as my eyes begin to bug out upon already being able to see off the end of the runway into the tundra!!

"That's why we left the flaps up! Now get ready. Okay.... *NOW!*"

And I place the flap handle in the first notch. The airspeed now registers a solid 40 MPH.

On a wing and a prayer . . . well, on a prayer, anyway.
At home in Fairbanks.

"Now see," says Dan. He is moving the control yoke back and forth, almost full travel, which only serves to move the nose of the airplane up and down slightly at this point. "Now ... see. Like I said. There's no way that is going to work *(uh-huh)* . . . now get ready to give me another notch."

In another 7 seconds, we are approaching the 3/4 mark of the runway. Dan calls for another ten degrees. As I extend the fowler flaps, the airspeed is tickling the mark halfway between fifty and sixty. My God, we are doomed, I'm sure.

But smilin' Dan once again starts working the control wheel, and this time is rewarded with the sound of the blaring stall horn and the nose wheel breaking contact with the ground.

But a quick, horrified glance out my right window confirms that, not only are the main wheels still firmly planted in the soft gravel, but this pig shows no indication of even getting light in her loafers yet. The end of the runway—as well as my life, I suspect—is coming up all to quickly, even at this ridiculous speed *(Oh Momma! I Love you. Goodbye! Oh, why didn't I ever learn to listen to my momma?)*

"The stall warning horn blares as my life flashes before my eyes."

What? What is the insane man saying? What? Yes. Yes, Dan. I can see that the %$#@ing airplane is "not quite ready to fly"! And I'm sorry to disagree with you, you aerodynamically deficient MORON ... but no! No! I don't believe it's getting close. What? What! Oh! The end of the runway's coming up?! Well, what the hell did you EXPECT, dammit?! JEEZUZ! I can't believe I let you kill me! What?

Oh. You want *FULL* flaps now?! Well sure! That'll really help! Let's add some MORE *drag* for cryin' out loud.

I bang the flap handle full down in anger, disgust, and self-pity; and after taking a final glance at the airspeed indicator, which has climbed to all of 62 MPH, I take one brief look at the last 250 feet or so of gravel over the top of the nose that leads undoubtedly to my early and unfortunate demise. Bracing my left arm firmly against the glare shield, I snap my head sideways against the window in frustration and closing my eyes with my right hand to cover them I wait for...THE END!

The stall warning horn goes on steady as my life flashes before my eyes —which at nineteen years of age doesn't even make for a long flash—and I lament that I never boinked my high school girlfriend, or her best friend. Or that cute little redhead down the street. In general I have a brief feeling of, *"I been robbed,"* in a sexual sort of way.

These thoughts are immediately and instantly replaced with a four word prayer (*"Oh God Forgive Me"*) and a sincere and heartfelt last hope (I assume) that I have "covered my ass" with that in lieu of a full "Act of Contrition" as I am, at present, feeling a little pressed for time. It's all over in just those few seconds.

But instead of the expected little "jump" off the lip at the end of the runway followed by the blackness, I realize the bouncing has . . . stopped?! But the stall horn is still blowing steady.

Wha- the- heck-

I spread two of my fingers apart, crack my right eye open and see the tundra rushing by no more than a dozen feet below me.

"We're alive! We're ALIVE!" I scream.

I do not know it at the time, but find out later that Stanley Senior (and Junior,) as well as the other villagers seated behind me, looked at each other with completely bewildered expressions, and later came to the conclusion that there must be something wrong with me!

Thirsty for more? Visit Cloudy's online store at: <u>www.clouddancer.org</u>

Tell him Cap'n Aux sent ya!

SECTION 4: Pilots of the Caribbean

—BEFORE—
Mallard formation during evacuation.
Note the telltale washboard swells of an approaching hurricane.
(See following story)

Gone with the Hurricane!

Our world turned upside down

I wrote most of this story shortly after experiencing Hurricane Hugo back in '89. When I first published it on the blog years later, it coincided with the very week that Hurricane Sandy devastated the Eastern U.S. Seaboard.

The timing was a freak coincidence, and in no way did I intend to detract from the many hardships and sufferings experienced by survivors and victims of other Hurricanes such as Sandy, Katrina and Ivan. This is merely my story.

I hope the rest of the "uninitiated" world will learn something here about living through a hurricane, and also about the madness, mayhem and lawlessness that follows . . .

PART I: THE EVACUATION

Hugo: there never was a hurricane more aptly named. It sounded like the neighborhood bully; a Hubert or Harold just wouldn't have cut it. And on September 16, 1989, Hugo, the bastard son of Mother Nature, picked a fight with my little airline.

I was flying for the Virgin Islands Seaplane Shuttle out of St. Croix, USVI. We were a modest but intrepid outfit in the spirit of the isles we served.

With five Grumman Mallard amphibian seaplanes and two land-based De Havilland Twin Otters, we ferried gawking tourists and locals alike over the turquoise waters, pristine coral reefs and lush jungles of the U.S. and British Virgin Islands, and Puerto Rico.

Yes, it was a job in paradise.

But it was about to become, "Paradise Lost."

"It was a job in paradise about to become, 'Paradise Lost'."

For much of the year, the Caribbean pilot can forecast weather as deftly as the seasoned meteorologist: mostly sunny, isolated showers, light easterly breeze, temperature upper seventies. But during hurricane season, the climate undergoes an evil, Jekyll-and-Hyde metamorphosis. Waves of weather, borne in the mid-Atlantic, sweep through the Antilles like the hands of a clock--and just as regularly. These fronts build momentum, sucking up moisture and energy from the warm Caribbean waters. Some of these systems hatch tropical storms; often they grow into hurricanes.

So it is, during this season, that the Caribbean pilot suspiciously eyes each wave of weather, anxiously chews his lip as winds build to hurricane speed, then frantically plots its westward course as it plows across the seas.

If the storm veers homeward, the evacuation begins.

Such was the case with the season of 1989. The enemy advanced, our forces retreated. We evacuated the humble fleet to PSY (Ponce, Puerto Rico.) As copilot Mike and I flew our Twin Otter across the Caribbean Sea, clouds rushed in at record speed. Thunderstorms popped up like acne on a teen. Below us a washboard of rhythmic ocean swells stretched to the horizon, warning of the approaching storm. We landed, lashed down the planes and took refuge in a nearby hotel. Our troops silently searched the skies for the Blitzkrieg.

It never came. We soon lost interest and headed for the officers' club (a local cantina.) The only damage sustained on that outing was a few rum hangovers; the only hurricane present was the one pounding in our heads.

So much for the storm preceding the Main Event.

Hugo came out to play.

We again evacuated, this time to San Juan. But only three planes were flyable at the time; the others were down for maintenance. What the heck, we figured, too much trouble to put them back together. The boy cried wolf last time, it'd probably be the same with Hugo. We'll take a chance. And shucks, the last time a major hurricane hit St. Croix was way back in 1928, right?

We flew above the ocean at 4,000 feet, and again saw the telltale washboard swells. They radiated like waves from a stone dropped in water. But this stone was two hundred miles wide.

We stuffed the planes into a giant, three-story hangar at SJU (San Juan International Airport.) One drawback: no hangar door. If the hurricane did indeed hit, and the winds blew from the south, the whole building—and its contents—would blow away like Dorothy's house to the land of Oz. We crossed our fingers.

—*BEFORE*—
Our Idyllic life was about to be turned upside down...

San Juan Flight Service Station was a bedlam of frantic meteorologists, anxious pilots and noisy reporters. All crowded in, straining to hear the latest scrap of news on Hugo's progress. Yes, he would hit; the Virgin Islands his first target. STX (Alexander Hamilton Airport, St. Croix), reported 80mph winds and rising. Then all contact was lost.

My guts churned. All I could do was pray for my girlfriend Julia who, unbeknownst to me, missed her flight in the last-minute confusion, and was left behind on the island to fend for herself.

—BEFORE—

Cap'n Aux savors his first real Captain's seat, in the 19-pax Twin Otter (complete with '80 hair and '70's mustache!)

Hugo slowed, and parked its blistering, 160 mph blender smack on top of St. Croix. We scurried to our hotel rooms and battened down the hatches.

The only eye closed that night was Hugo's . . . and it closed in on us.

"The only eye closed that night was Hugo's . . . and it closed in on us."

Remember those lunchtime outings to the airport, sitting under the departure path and listening to the ear-splitting roar of jets overhead? Well, that's what it sounds like in the middle of a hurricane—for eight solid hours. And through the din you hear glass shatter, cars crash and tin roofs rip away. And you pray that your roof isn't next.

The sleepless night dragged on to morning. In a feeble attempt at distraction from the onslaught, we played cards. Being stuck on the ground floor of a hotel only 2 blocks from the beach, our biggest fear was floods and tsunamis. Mercifully, our ground turned out to be high enough.

—*LEFT BEHIND*—
Stranded in St. Croix in a glass house atop a hill. Julia is seated on left.

—*BEFORE*—
The gorgeous Grumman Mallard amphib highlighted by a full moon . . .

Finally, that afternoon, the winds died to a safe speed. We cautiously emerged, anxious to see how the planes had fared. All feared the worst.

We drove to the airport, forging knee-deep gully washers and swerving around downed power lines, tumbled trees, battered cars.

"With all contact lost with the island, we took off to scout the ruins."

San Juan Luis Munoz Airport was a mess. Airplanes lay strewn haphazard about the ramp. In all, 22 aircraft destroyed. One DC-3 lay inverted atop another plane, its type indistinguishable. I chewed my nails as we neared the hangar. The top two floors were caved in, but otherwise the hangar was largely intact. Our hopes jumped. The hurricane, it seemed, had swerved north before reaching San Juan. Except for a dinged wing tip, our three planes survived.

The next day, Chief Pilot Rudy deemed it safe enough to take off and scout the ruins of St. Croix. All contact was still lost with the entire island. I feared for Julia's safety. While I knew she had hunkered down with our friends in a concrete pillbox of a house, in a hurricane anything could happen.

—AFTER—
The twisted remains of a light twin Piper Aztec.

With no airport info nor weather data for STX, we took off. We only took the two Mallards, as Rudy figured we could land in the bay if the airport was trashed.

It was a flight I'll never forget.

I gazed out the window at the most beautiful sunset I've ever seen; Hugo's final, sarcastic farewell to the newly orphaned islands. The photo I snapped of our companion Mallard flying formation is one of the most gorgeous photos I've ever taken.

My original "Cap'n Aux" logo, borne of a hurricane.

As I marveled at the fantastic sight, and contemplated its grim irony, I couldn't help but think that the sun was also setting on our little airline in paradise.

SECTION 5: Adventure Travel

The Girl, the Sold Watch, and Everything—A Thai Adventure

Dedicated to Team Aloha & the Cheese Gang

This is one of my all-time favorite stories. For me it represents—in a humorous way—the essence of traveling in a 3rd world country.

One of my favorite things to do is toss a few clothes in a backpack, throw a dart at a map of the world, and show up in that spot the next day. Bonus points for finding a place with no internet, no paved roads and no English speakers. While Thailand is more developed and tourist-oriented than some neighboring countries in the region, its culture is still quite alien to Westerners.

Forgive the strange title: it's a takeoff on John D. McDonald's humorous novel entitled, ***The Girl, the Gold Watch, and Everything***. McDonald is perhaps best known for his novel-turned-movie, *Cape Fear*. He is also the author of one of my favorite series characters, Travis McGee. Justin Reed, the troubled teen orphan star of my ***Code Name: Dodger*** spy series, takes several cues from Travis, and if you like author Carl Hiaasen, you'll love the Travis McGee series.

Eeeeeeeeeeeeeeeeeeeeeeeeeeeeeeeeeeeeeeeeeee
went our little scooter, put-putting at full hamster motor speed to haul our two *Farong* (Westerner) tushies up the winding Thailand hillside.

Eyes squinted in determination and tongue chewed in concentration, I fishtailed up the "wrong" (left) side of the twisting, 2-lane, rice noodle road. Blasting their horns in warning, overcrowded buses, Tuk Tuks and scooters whizzed by, from both ways—in Thailand, traffic lanes, lights and laws are only a friendly suggestion.

"In Thailand, laws are only a friendly suggestion."

My travel buddy Lisa did an admirable job of not squealing in terror . . . too often. But her fingers digging into my sides told a different story. If her nails had not been already gnawed to the nubs, my flanks would have been shredded into fish gills.

"800 baht!" the street vendor's voice still rang in my ears, in concert with the whine of the hamster motor and horn shrieks. "It's good watch, Boss! For you, good price!"

"For you, Boss, good price!"

That line. *For you, good price!* Do they hammer that line into every street hawker the world 'round? Of course, it invites haggle, and after three weeks I had once again mastered the Art of the Deal, rather than the standard American reply of, "Duh, okay!"

My previous watch died, appropriately, on Day One of our trip. I happily ditched the watch, and my obsession with time thereof, for the rest of our Thai sojourn. But now, with airline time tables looming a scant few days away for my 30-hour, 10-time zone trek home, I began to once again hanker for a reliable, if not too flashy, time piece.

As a pilot, I'm picky about my watch. But I've never bought into the silly, thousand-dollar wonders marketed as "You're not a real pilot unless you have a *Breitling* like good ol' Captain John Travolta."

The Girl...

More bells, dials, whistles, and aerodynamic gleaming alloy than his Gulfstream II. Guaranteed to send the airport X-ray scanner into convulsions. All status symbol and flash. But does it actually tell time?

Me, I go for practical. Dual time—one digital, one analog — to keep me upright while zigzagging the time zones; day and date prominently displayed; an alarm and, well, ok, a stopwatch if you must. Not too big, not too flashy. $32.99 at Walmart.

Our travel mates, Brian and Beth, lean that other way, though. To wit, Lisa and I politely tagged along as they scoured the Phuket Island vendors in the city of Patong for the ultimate deal on Rolex knock-offs . . . or Folex, as we came to mockingly call 'em.

"Eyes darting furtively, he smuggled us into his secret back room."

Eyes darting furtively about, the winning vendor smuggled us into his super secret back room and plied Brian with only the "best of the best." A veteran of Thai travels, Brian talked him down from 6000 to 2700 baht — $90 for two pieces of the finest, flashiest junk the 3rd World had to offer.

From 800 baht, I'd talked my vendor down to 350. $12. Not bad for a novice Farong, but still more than a local, or even Brian, would pay. I didn't mind. One-third the price of Walmart. *Good price, Boss!*

SOLD!

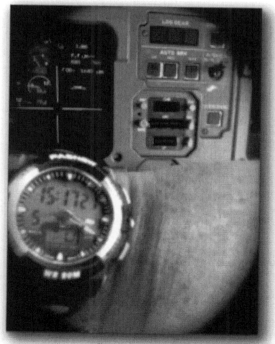

The Sold Watch...

Eeeeeeeeeeeeeeeeeeeeeeeeeeeeeeeeeeeeeeeeeeeeee

So why was our Little Engine That Barely Could struggling to haul our Farong derrieres up over the hill and back to the mayhem of Patong?

Because, two hours later, the big and little hands still displayed 10:20 a.m. — the exact time of my smokin' watch deal. Unless we were trapped in a wormhole, my $12 wonder watch had stopped working.

> *"More bells, dials and gleaming alloy than John Travolta's Gulfstream. But does it actually tell time?"*

Or, to be more precise, had never worked to begin with. The analog hands, that is. The digital LED portion reported, correctly, the current local time as 12:32.

Much to my dismay, I knew, we were most certainly *not* trapped in a time warp.

So, reluctantly ripping ourselves away from our beach chairs and Chang beers (80 baht, good price!), Lisa and I zigzagged our way back to the point of sale.

Knowing that my street vendor may suddenly close for lunch if he spied me approaching with a return, I surreptitiously slipped up to the stall pretending to be a new customer. I was immediately greeted with another, "For you, good price, Boss!"

...and, well, you know...

Smiling, I held up the defunct watch. "No good, Boss!" I replied.

Deer in headlights look. With surprisingly minimal hassle, I got a new, if different, watch — Thai street dealers never seem to have the same two time pieces, but rather a mishmash of stock.

"Instruction manual?" I asked. Digging through a stack of manuals, the boy thrust a random booklet into my hand. At least the thing had the same manufacturer name as was printed on the face of the watch.

Eeeeeeeeeeeeeeeeeeeeeeeeeeeeeeeeeeeeeeeeeeeeeee

Back over the hill we put-putted, my new wonder piece gleaming on my left wrist.

Did I mention April is Thailand's hottest, muggiest month? Think Atlanta summer plus ten degrees temp *and* humidity.

Drenched in sweat, we jumped into the pristine water for a few minutes' respite before settling back in our beach chairs and ordering up a coupla new, nearly cold, Changs.

Still skeptical about the new watch, I checked the analog dials. Still happily tic-tocking away! That's when I noticed the digital part. Foggy with seawater, with the LED display all smeared!

"Nothing short of a $12 watch could rip me away from this slice of heaven!

"Eeeeeeeeeeeeeeeeeeeeeeeeeeeeeeeeeeeeeeeeeeeee

Deer in headlights. Unsure, the young vendor nervously glanced at his boss. "Here," the stall owner said, thrusting a new time piece into my hand. "Here is better watch! You go now and no come back!"

"No worries, mate!" I replied, knowing that, functional or no, I was not hauling our kiesters back over the mountain and away from our beachside Changs for yet another $12 piece of dysfunctional junk.

Back on our little patch of sand-strewn paradise, dripping wet with cool seawater and clasping new semi-chilled beers, the pilot in me ran through a mental checklist, something like this:

— — — —

3rd World Time Piece Functionality Checklist:

Analog hands tick-ticking test —	*Check!*
Post-swim digital LED test —	*Check!*
Nightlight luminosity test —	*Check!*
Day, Date, Year reasonably correct test —	*Check!*

3rd World Time Piece Checklist —	*Complete!*

— — — —

I am proud to report that, after an entire week, multiple time zone crossings, now half a world away and back in the office at 35,000' enroute to STL, my new timepiece keeps on *tickin'!* As the setting sun reflects off the clouds below, my Thai wonder still precisely reads the time as 10:20 am.

WTF?!?!

"Eeeeeeeeeeeeeeeeeeeeeeeeeeeeeeeeeeeeeeeeeeeee"

P.S. — Oh, ya, and Thailand has lots of cool places to see, eat, ride elephants, snorkel, hike, rock climb, party and stuff. Lotsa giant gold Buddha's, cool temples and the like . . .

But you can figure that out by reading your Lonely Planet guide book.

SECTION 6: By Popular Demand
A few of my most popular works

Zen & the Art of Aircraft Maintenance

No flight's complete until the paperwork is done!

While not technically in the *There I Wuz!* category, this post is consistently one of the top <u>capnaux.com</u> posts of all time, probably due to its similarity to the popular book, *Zen and the Art of Motorcycle Maintenance.* Or, maybe folks just love a good laugh. In any case, it's a hoot to read!

**Pilot's maintenance write-up (Squawk):
"Something loose in the cockpit."
Mechanic's corrective action (CA):
"Something tightened in the cockpit."**

If you're any kind of aviation buff, you've most likely seen this and other gems in a popular email of funny aircraft maintenance write-ups. If not, I'll take that as an excuse to plagiarize a few more here for your pleasure.

**Squawk: "Aircraft handles funny."
CA: "Aircraft told to straighten up, fly right, and be serious."**

Maintenance write-ups, or "Squawks" in pilot parlance, are a daily occurrence for pilots. When you're trying to keep safely in the sky a man-made bird with a million parts, well, that means a million and one things can go wrong. Fortunately, a century's progress in aircraft design has rendered modern airliners extremely safe; failures of the catastrophic kind are nearly unheard of. But hassles of the minor and mundane kind, the equivalent of the knob popping off the radio in your '03 Prius, are an every day occurrence. While you may be able to live without that knob (I've been using the remote control in my '98 Celica for the past year), every single airliner's maintenance issue, no matter how trivial, must be addressed before flight.

**Squawk: "Number Three Engine missing."
CA: "Number Three Engine found on right wing after brief search."**

But you wouldn't want to delay, let alone cancel, a flight for, say, a broken toilet seat.

Enter the MEL, or Minimum Equipment List. The FAA allows airliners to hurtle through the stratosphere with a myriad of broken parts, such as toilet seats, until those minor bits can be fixed while overnighting at a maintenance base.

**Squawk: "Mouse in radio stack."
CA: "Cat installed in radio stack."**

You know how, when you take your Prius to the mechanic, that *whee whee whee* sound it was making suddenly fixes itself? Same thing happens on a plane. ("But I swear, Frank, that radio was going *screeeech!* a minute ago!") There's nothing more frustrating to a pilot than receiving as a Corrective Action: "Could not duplicate; returned to service." Worse, I've had my share of rookie squawks based on my lack of intimate knowledge of the airplane. ("Uh, lady, that *chunk chunk chunk* you're hearing and feeling is called a 'flat tire'.")

Once, fresh on the Airbus, I wrote up the APU (Auxiliary Power Unit) when I couldn't get it to start—only to find out that you had to first turn on the Batteries to help power it up. Uh . . . duh! Now, after 20 years on the A320, I'm more than comfy on "Fifi's" flight deck, though she still finds little ways to rise up and make me humble again. That APU write-up, for example, is not just for rookies. Even vets fall for it from time to time, when the Starbucks across from the gate hasn't opened yet.

Er, um. . . so I'm told . . . .

Squawk: "Evidence of hydraulic leak on right main landing gear."
CA: "Evidence removed."

For the hi-tech Airbus, 90% of my squawks are quickie fixes. Reset a couple circuit breakers, do a quick byte test, and you're off and running. But little things often do have the habit of snowballing into big things. Hence the perpetually frustrating "another ten minutes and we'll be underway" PA you hear a dozen times before actual door close. All we pilots know is what our mechanics tell us, so please don't kill the messenger. And please, please, *please* don't take it out on the flight attendants, either! They've had a long day, too, and wanna get there just as badly as you do. We're all in this boat together.

Squawk: "Dead bugs on windshield."
CA: "Live bugs on order."

While we all have our airline delay horror stories, my personal record was eight hours—count 'em, eight!—hours stuck on on the plane, doors closed, on the tarmac in Newark.* While our original maintenance delay only put us back 30 minutes, it was just long enough to ground-stop all traffic as a slow-moving wall of thunderstorms leisurely strolled overhead. Our flight took off four minutes before our "drop-dead" time (i.e., max legal duty time) expired. And then came the five hour flight to Las Vegas.

Squawk: "Test flight OK, except autoland very rough."
CA: "Autoland not installed on this aircraft."

So, your ace mechanics swooped in on the plane and did their magic. You're all patched up and ready to launch, right? Well, not exactly. No flight is ready until the paperwork is done. While a circuit breaker reset might take two minutes, the paperwork takes at least ten. For, close on the heels of the airline pilot's mantra of "Safety First," is "Charlie Yankee Alpha—Cover Your A$$." The FAA can smell a dubious paper trail from FL390, so it is imperative that that toilet seat's Green Card is filled out in triplicate, "i's" dotted and "t's" crossed, signed and stamped by the mechanic, entered into the memory banks and approved by Maintenance Control back at Company

HQ, and sent via ACARS message (a fancy term for onboard email) to the cockpit. After that, the Company dispatcher must amend the flight manifest to include the broken toilet seat, calculate its aerodynamic effects on fuel burn, and ACARS that to the cockpit as well, where it must, ultimately, be christened as safe by the Captain.

God forbid a poor, unsuspecting passenger sit down in the lav and suffer the consequences!

Squawk: "Whining sound heard on engine shutdown."
CA: "Pilot removed from aircraft."

This incident took place years before the "Passenger Bill of Rights" was passed. One poor couple onboard missed their own Vegas wedding, and sheepishly asked if the Captain of the Ship could perform the ceremony onboard. Oh, how I wish I had!

Top 10 Downers of an Airline Pilot Career

This post came in as the most popular of 2013, and understandably so.

Believe it or not, this really is a *There I Wuz!*-type adventure, as it truly puts you in an airline pilot's shoes.

Through my blog, novels, photos and videos, I strive to inspire the "chairborne" and avgeek, and fuel our up-and-coming generation of pilots with the passion of flight. While encouraging them to pursue their dream just like I did, I nevertheless want them to come into this business with open eyes. Even in the best of times, the airline life can be brutal.

Here's a reality check for all you dreamers!

It Ain't All Fun 'n Games, you know!

People are always asking me what the life of an airline pilot is really like.

To many, it all seems to all be glitz 'n glamor. Exotic locales. Bitchin' airplanes. Smokin' hot flight attendants at your beck and call . . .

Not to mention the "Best office view in the world!"

But is that truly the case?

At the risk of sounding whiny or nit-picky, I will attempt to show you some of the downside of this profession—the warts, if you will. . .

Now, I know that, no matter what I choose to mention, many of you aspiring pilot types will say, "Gee, I'd give my left (insert body part here) to have your problems!"

Well . . . I fully understand! Been there, thought that!

Even so, I want you to come into this business with open eyes. And for you "chairborne" types, I'd like to give you a better feel for "life on the road" (and in the sky.)

Read on . . .

"Holidays? What's that?"

1.) Schedule: You're gone from home half a week at a time.

When I get home after a 4-day trip, I find my life has been going on without me. It always takes at least a day just to catch up. No time for rest till the mail's opened, the bills are paid, the cat box is cleaned, the sink unclogged and the trees trimmed.

And don't even get me started on the laundry . . .

Oh, and, my vicious attack cat Tarzan scolds me for half a day as punishment for abandoning him for so long!

Vicious attack cat Tarzan, post-scolding.

2.) Schedule 2.0: "9 to 5, M-F" does not exist.

You will fly redeyes. You will fly Oh-Dark-Thirty departures. You may even do both in the same trip!

Crossing multiple time zones will wreak havoc on your body. By the very nature of this business, you will age faster than everybody else.

And no matter how "senior" your schedule, getting adequate rest is always a challenge.

"Redeyes & Oh-dark-thirty departures—in the same trip!"

FAA minimum rest requirements help, but they are just that—minimal. Many airlines schedule right up to these limits. Flight attendants have it even worse, with much less restrictive rest requirements.

3.) Schedule 3.0—or, "Holidays? What's that?"

You will be gone from home, sitting alone in a hotel room on all major holidays, little Sally's 4th birthday party, and Timmy's championship Little League game.

After 23 years at my company, I have yet to hold full weekends or Christmas off. As a first officer, you may briefly taste a senior moment, but the calling of the Left Seat is far too strong.

And then you're at the bottom of the next pile.

"If you want job security, shun flying & take up acting!"

4.) Enough about the Schedule, already! How about that great paycheck?

People often swoon over a pilot's seemingly exorbitant hourly pay rate. But what they don't realize is that a pilot is paid only for the time the plane is moving. You will work long hours, 10-12 hours a day or more, and get paid for less than half of that time.

Time between flights, even though you are busy planning, preflighting, briefing the crew or dealing with mechanical issues, are done completely gratis.

5.) Paycheck 2.0: Yeah, Cap'n Aux, but it's still pretty stellar! Right?

Hmm, yeah, about that. Pilots' paychecks are a fraction of what they once were—up to 60% lower than 20 years ago.

On top of that, the left seat of a major airline represents the Holy Grail of aviation. After spending many years and tens of thousands of dollars on education and flight training, only a fraction of a fraction of pilots will ever see it. And nearly every other flying job pays peanuts.

"After spending tens of thousands of $ only a fraction make it."

Pilots are a dime a dozen. That "looming pilot shortage" has been "looming" for 30 years! And, all aviation outfits know that most pilots are merely building time to move on to a major. But even some of those lucky enough to snag the right seat of an airliner could still qualify for food stamps.

Moreover, every six months, airline pilots must pass a rigorous medical exam. Flunk once, and you could be out for life!

Ding an airplane or bust a single FAA rule . . . same result!

As I've always said: if you want a secure career, shun flying and become an actor!

6.) Paycheck 3.0: What Goes Up . . .

Unlike most professions, pilots cannot make lateral moves. Quit, get fired, or the airline goes "Tango Uniform" *(Pilot code for "dead". The words that Tango and Uniform stand for are left as an exercise to the reader)*, and you start at the bottom at the next airline. You could have been a senior 747 Captain at Brand X Airways, pulling down well into the 6-digits, but now you're a lowly reserve FO (First Officer) at Brand Y . . . on food stamp wages!

Personally, for the first decade of my career, my paycheck looked like the flight of a Yoyo.

Nowadays, if you're experienced enough, you may be able to find a fairly lucrative, 2-3 year Captain contract overseas. China in particular is really heating up. (I came a hair's breadth from taking one there.) But you will be saying good-bye to your loved ones for weeks, even months, at a time.

7.) Relationships? What's that?

Once upon a time, a girlfriend complained, "I can't handle this long distance relationship!"—even though we lived in the same town. It shocked me into realizing: As long as I fly for a living, I will always have "long distance relationships."

The nature of this business demands a helluva lotta trust from both parties. Remember, you're sleeping in hotel rooms thousands of miles away, several times a week—and they're home alone.

This career will create stress in any marriage or relationship!

8.) Layovers—Slam-click!

Rome, Paris, London, New York . . . exciting, exotic locales! Who would not want to visit these amazing places on a regular basis?

Yes, any one of our layovers has the potential for adventure. Occasionally, you gel with a crew, and all of you go out and see the sights, or party till dawn. Those are some of my fondest memories.

But even the most exciting of world destinations get old after the 20th or 30th time. And who among us can get excited about our 30-hour Detroit layover, especially in the middle of a blizzard?

After a long day of fighting through the storms and turbulence, sometimes you just wanna trudge to your hotel room and *Slam-click!* (*Slam-clicker: An airline crew member that doesn't want to do anything but slam their hotel room door and click the lock shut!*)

Oh, and speaking of down time, you know those annoying, hours-long layovers you get between your connections? We have them too—nearly every day. It is not uncommon to sit 3 hours or more at an airport, waiting for your next flight. We call this, airport appreciation time. And our airports get get plenty of crew appreciation.

Yes, I'm complaining here about free time, but I can tell you first hand: long sit times create fatigue. And the F word is poison to pilots.

Last year, CareerCast named "Airline Pilot" 3rd most stressful job—behind 1. Enlisted Military, and 2. Military General.

9.) Deadheads—Not exactly Grateful

(Deadhead: Riding in back as a passenger from Point A to Point B to work another flight from Point B to C.)

Depending on the airline, some pilots get paid 1/2 or no pay for these flights. All too often, you get stuck in a coach middle seat between two ginormous, sweaty Sumo wrestlers. OK, so we all get stuck there from time to time . . . but doing this every week gets old mighty fast. Jumpseating is worse: If you're lucky, you'll get a seat in back!

10.) Commuting—or, Home? What's that?

(Commuting: Riding as a passenger—either in the cabin or cockpit jumpseat—between Home & work.)

Let's go full circle, back to Number 1—being "gone from home."

As you chase your airline career, be prepared to move—again and again and again.

I spent my first 22 years on this planet in Arizona. In the next ten & beyond, I lived in: Juneau, Alaska, St. Thomas & St. Croix, U.S. Virgin Islands, Denver, Colorado, Washington, DC, Albuquerque, New Mexico, and back to Arizona—several times.

The moment you put money down on your new house in Boise, ID, your airline will transfer you to Buffalo, NY. The moment your first child is born in Seattle, you'll snag that dream job in Florida.

You have two options: move, or commute across the country twice a week on an airplane jumpseat. (See my post, "Around the World in 80 Jumpseats.")

If you choose to commute from home, you'll most likely be renting a one-room "crash pad" with half a dozen other pilot-commuters at your airline's assigned base. Have fun with that!

By the way, at my airline, at least 40% of pilots are commuters . . .

That reminds me of a funny story:

We used to fly a lot of redeyes in and out of KLAS (Las Vegas.) At about 2 or 3 in the morning, all these flight crews would deadhead back to home base on the last flight. We would have dozens of pilots and flight attendants onboard, sometimes more crew than passengers! We dubbed this flight, The Crew Hauler.

One time, a befuddled passenger, mystified by all these pilots riding in the back of the plane, asked me, "Do you guys just ride in back because you love flying so much?"

Well, I wouldn't go that far . . .

But, despite my profession's many ugly warts, the dirty little secret is . . .

it's still the greatest job in the world!

Besides . . .

—Christmas with the kids can be rescheduled;

—Families or significant others can come along on those exotic overnights (Marry me, fly free!)

—All that down time is good for a hobby or 2nd job (where do you think I get all that free time to write my books 'n blog?);

—Find the right, understanding spouse, and your "long distance relationship" can be a rewarding one. After all, absence really does make the heart grow fonder.

—As a pilot, you have the freedom to work and live in different parts of the world. With a wonderful home and family to return to, even crash pads and commuting can be endured.

Most important of all: as you viciously claw your way up the aviation food chain, never forget to enjoy the ride.

As comedian Louis C.K. says it, "You're sitting in a chair . . . *in the sky!*"

(AND getting PAID for it!)

SECTION 7: Love, Laughs . . . and Tears in the Sky

Photo of fellow Formation Blogger Ron Rapp, his lovely wife, and their lovely Pitts Special. Visit him at Rapp.org

The Loon is a Harsh Mistress
The Pilot's Dysfunctional Love Affair

My first Valentine's post for *Adventures of Cap'n Aux*, this is the story of how I came to flying. It's also a good discourse on the passion we all share for aviation. More than just a hobby, it can easily turn into an obsession—one that can, and has, caused divorces.

Another strange title, taken from another favorite book: Robert Heinlein's sci fi masterpiece, T*he Moon is a Harsh Mistress*.

Yes, the airplane may be the most powerful love of our lives, but she too can be a harsh mistress.

"For once you have tasted flight, you will walk the earth with your eyes turned skywards.
For there you have been and there you will long to return."
—Leonardo da Vinci

Ask any pilot how they started flying, and you will hear a love story.
One just like mine:
From age 5, I dreamed of flying. Scanned the skies. Built model airplanes. Along with my buddy Alan, doodled dogfights during math class. Thrilled at the occasional trip to the airport and practically peed my pants to actually fly. To this day, I remember verbatim the conversation I had—at age 8—with the Hughes Airwest pilots in the cockpit of their Boeing 737.

"My soul is in the sky."
— William Shakespeare, "A Midsummer Night's Dream"

When I was 14, I announced my intent to buy a hang glider. Dad said, "Son, if you have the money, you can buy a hang glider." Little did he know that this flying-obsessed boy had been saving up lawn mowing allowance for the past three years! I promptly bought a used Rogallo wing for $430. I diligently took the ground school, aced the tests, and was thoroughly prepared. Nevertheless, the flight school, perhaps wisely, made me wait another year, till I was 15, to fly. And, God bless his soul, my father honored his words, crossed his fingers and let this fledgling chick spread his wings.

It changed my life. The euphoric feeling was a drug that I would pursue for the rest of my life.

Me and the venerable De Havilland Beaver. The ship that launched a novel.

Fly. Flying. *To Fly.*

Shortly thereafter, I visited the Smithsonian Air & Space Museum, which included a viewing of the classic IMAX film, *"To Fly!"* Like few other earthbound media, it captured for me the sheer joy and grandeur and magic that is flying.

*To Fly...*Hearing those words still give me goosebumps.

From that moment on, I was determined to make a life for myself in the sky.

Death And Ex's

"All at once in love again with this painful bittersweet lovely thing called flight."
— Richard Bach, *"A Gift of Wings"*

While an Ex or two may have had her suspicions of a fling with a flight attendant, the true culprit would be my long-term love affair with "Fifi," my A320. Today, her graceful looks, sleek, sexy lines and loving, yet quirky and unforgiving personality are my obsession.

Indeed, I believe more airline-related divorces can be traced to this plain plane obsession than sexual flings. Often, the plain plane-obsessed pilot comes home from his trip, pecks his wife on the cheek, repacks, and is off to the weekend fly-in. Football widows got nuthin' on airplane widows.

Southwest Airlines captain Larry K. retires.

Accountants, firemen, even physicians can retire and live to a ripe old age. But, despite the relatively youthful forced-retirement age of 65, the pilot-retiree often augers in within scant months or years. I am convinced that this is because, inside, he is heartbroken. He has lost the Love of his Life; his harsh mistress of 30-some years has traded him in for a newer model. Oh, he may have dabbled with his own Cessna 182 during his brief twilight years, but it's like trading the Supermodel for the cleaning lady. He has lost his purpose, his identity, a large chunk of his core personality.

> *"Love.*
> *Love keeps her in the air when she oughta fall down,*
> *tells you she's hurting 'fore she keens.*
> *Makes her a home."*
> —Captain Malcomb Reynolds, "Serenity"

Mal had his *Serenity*. Kirk had his *Enterprise*. And I have my *Fifi*.

Fifi is my spaceship.

From her glass cockpit at 39,000', on a moonless night I can gaze out the window at the lights of Planet Earth as they meld with the Milky Way, and imagine being in command of a starship cruising at Warp Speed.

Cap'n Aux and Fifi.

MCCOY: Well, I doubt seriously if there's any kind of love antidote we can give the Captain for the *Enterprise*.
SPOCK: In this particular instance, Doctor, I agree with you.
KIRK: Mr. Sulu, ahead Warp Factor Two.

—**Star Trek**, *Elaan of Troyius* (paraphrased)

I savor these fleeting years, when I and my harsh mistress are perfectly content.

The Poker Game That Launched My Career

This is one of the first stories I ever wrote for *Adventures of Cap'n Aux*. I think it kind of sets the tone that I often strive for: an adventurous, true tale, told in a humorous way, that speaks of some serendipitous reality. This is the quintessential tortoise-and-hare tale, albeit with a surprising twist: I daresay that, had I *not* suffered an excruciating hangover that fateful day, I may not be here to tell you my tall tales!

"It's mind-boggling to realize there were simple decisions that ultimately determined your life."

It's mind-boggling—"uncanny," as my dad would have said—to look back on life and realize that there were single, seemingly innocuous decisions that ultimately determined the path that your life took. I'm not talking about the deliberate life decisions we try to make—marry or move on? Bear, abort or adopt? Aeronautical Engineer, English/Japanese Major, or Acting degree? *(Believe it or not, I seriously considered each of these degrees!)* How ironic that most of these important forks in life's road come within +/- the age of maximum arrogance and minimum experience—yes, I'm talking about the Golden Age of 18!

Ultimately, I decided on Aero Engineer, thinking it would boost my airline career prospects—until my buddy got hired by a major airline two years before me with a degree in . . . *Photography*. So much for the deliberate decisions.

No, I'm not talking about those. I'm talking about the seemingly simple, *serendipitous* decisions that, in retrospect, define the very essence of your life. Brake instead of push the yellow light, and miss a semi barreling through the intersection. Right instead of left, land a random job that becomes a career. Go to the bank instead of Starbucks, and meet the love of your life.

Looking back, I was flabbergasted (thanks Grandma Laura, for that word!) to realize that the essence of my career, the innocuous event that ultimately defined the path my life was to take, was . . . a poker game.

Fresh out of college, I found myself stuck. While attending college at Arizona State University, I had been flight instructing—the standard issue entry-level job for wanna-be, non-military pilot types. While it literally flew circles 'round the standard college McDonald's or waiter job (though perhaps not the way-cool bartender job,) it had put me in a rut.

"I was so confident that I quit both flying jobs."

At age 24, I had a BS degree and 2,200 hours of flying. Impressive. Most impressive. But I was not a Jedi yet. The vast majority of my time was flight instructing in single-engine Cessna 152's. I needed twin-engine time. And turboprop time. And instrument time. And, ultimately, jet time. But each rung on the aviation ladder comes with its own "Catch 22": you can't *get* the time without already *having* the time.

In addition to flight instructing, I had bagged my first "real" aviation job: flying charters. The bread and butter of the operation was the ubiquitous Grand Canyon tour in the mighty Cessna 210. Turbocharged, top 'o the line, a favorite of pilots. But still only a single-engine piston.

I was in a rut, and I knew it.

But then, opportunity fell into my lap. An outfit specializing in "flightseeing" tours out of GCN (Grand Canyon Airport) was hiring first officers for the mighty Twin Otter, a two-engine, two-pilot turboprop, with a whopping 19 passenger seats. This was my chance! My lucky break! With my six years of GCN flying, surely I was a shoe-in!

Like 18 other prospective pilot-candidates, I showed up at Day 1 of GCN Airways' week-long ground school awash with the enthusiasm of bagging a REAL "airline" job–certainly the springboard to the fabled Left Seat of a major airline!

I admit, I showed up cocky. Mighty cocky. I had three times more flight hours of every other candidate. When they informed us that only half the class would be hired, I felt sorry for those rookies around me who would no doubt get the pink slip.

So confident was I in my new calling, that I had quit both flight instructing and charter flying jobs.

Grandma Laura to
Lil' Cap'n Aux:
"Do what you want and
never worry what others think!"

The week of ground school flew by, a flurry of aircraft systems, procedures, company policies . . . and parties. While those other bores from class spent their nights diligently studying, I—in classic, tortoise and hare fashion—drank rum with my buddy Ramon, a GCN bus tour driver whom I'd met on one of our countless sojourns.

And then, on Saturday, came the final exam. At 8 am sharp, we would test on our knowledge of said systems, policies and procedures.

The night before, I went to Ramon's poker game.

I had a marvelous time. I cleaned out Ramon and his buddies, to the tune of $18 and change. The perfect end to a boring week of ground school!

> *"I made it to the Final Exam a little late.*
> *And more than a little hungover…"*

I made it to the test a little late—and more than a little hungover. The questions seemed a little harder than I thought necessary, and I guessed a little more than I probably should have.

It was only after I turned in my test that I got the shocking news: hiring was based STRICTLY on test performance, *not* on experience!

And when the results came out in the afternoon, I missed the last slot by 1/2 a point.

One. Half. Of. One. !#$%@$%&. *Point!*

Shellshocked, I watched in stunned silence as each of my winning classmates proudly stepped forward to accept their test—and the handshake welcoming them to the company.

Ego thoroughly thrashed, I limped home, a long, five-hour drive to Mom and Dad's.

"No job. No prospects. No career. In the poker game of life, I lost."

No job. No prospects. No career.

That $18 and change barely paid for my gas home. In the poker game of life, I'd lost the hand. Oh, if only I'd studied that fateful Friday night! I had only myself to blame.

Despite my best efforts to the contrary, however, it turned out that I'd won the pot. For, shortly thereafter, I got a phone call from my college buddy Kevin that would change my life. And launch my career.

Three days later, I found myself flying the Alaskan bush. An amazing experience full of *There I wuz!* stories that led me, inexorably and ironically, straight into the Left Seat of a Twin Otter—in the spectacular Virgin Islands, no less.

But that's another tale.

Flying a Fallen Hero

Published on NYCAviation

Dedicated to the memory of Sr. Airman Dustin Owens.

Sr. Airman Owens' casket is loaded aboard for his final flight.

This is one of my proudest and most intense works.

NYCAviation.com published it for their Memorial Day 2014 article, and it was also chosen to be the lead story in the pilot-writer anthology, *Skywriting* (theskywriterpress.com.)

If your eyes don't soak the page with tears, that's ok: mine do every time I read it.

"Like the Tomb of the Unknown Soldier, he was ours. He was us."

I recently experienced one of the greatest—and most heart-rending—honors a modern airline pilot can have: Captaining a flight that is transporting a fallen soldier to his final resting place.

Escorting the hero was a military honor guard consisting of two of the soldier's comrades, and two young Marines. Also onboard were the man's father and a lovely, devastated young woman—girlfriend? Wife? Sister? I never found out. I never learned the soldier's name, either. Or his rank. Or how or where he died.

But it didn't matter. Because, like the Tomb of the Unknown Soldier, he was ours. He was us.

Comrades and Honor Guard salute the Fallen . . .

As soon as our preflight duties were finished, I asked the gate agents to allow the party onboard. They were escorted to the ramp, where they presided over a short ceremony as the casket was loaded into the forward cargo hold. Simple, precise and crisp, the military detail saluted the casket then made a sharp about face to march away, reminding me of the Missing Man Formation often flown by jet fighters.

...and then crisply march away...

"For six hours as we crossed the country, I contemplated my speech."

For six hours as we crossed the country, I contemplated my speech. As Captain of the flight, I was expected to say a few words upon arrival. At Top of Descent, I took a deep breath and keyed the PA:

"Ladies and Gentlemen, this is your Captain speaking. I'd like you to pay special attention to this announcement. (pause) Today we have the great, great honor of escorting one of our fallen soldiers to his final resting place.

"Also on board, you may have noticed, is a military honor guard as well as family and loved ones of the deceased. I would like to personally request that, upon arriving at the gate, out of respect for our fallen hero, you remain seated as the party deplanes to meet their loved one plane-side."

And for his loved ones, I saved the best for last . . .

"And to those of you worried about connections, I would like to say that we are arriving thirty minutes early. That is because Air Traffic Control, aware of our status as an escort flight, cleared us 'Direct to Destination', in honor of our precious cargo. (deep breath, trying desperately not to choke up)

Ladies and Gentlemen, in my 30-plus years of flying, I have never witnessed such a gesture."

It was true. Despite pushing back from a major hub airport during rush hour, Ground Control cleared us straight to the runway, Tower immediately cleared us for takeoff, and Center direct to his final resting place.

It was my leg. I am proud to say that, in honor of the fallen, I was able to make one of my smoothest-ever "greaser" landings, and rolled quietly down and off the runway to the gate.

The entire cabin was quiet and still as the solemn party proceeded off the plane. I emerged from the cockpit just in time for the father, with tears in his eyes, whisper to me, "Thank you."

"It was an honor," I replied. "Take care, sir."

The party had another brief ceremony plane-side as the coffin was loaded onto a specially-painted black tug and cart and driven off-airport.

God paints a gorgeous sunset to welcome the Fallen to his final resting place.

Needless to say, the mood among the crew was somber and reflective.

That was, until a small girl, no more than four, marched up to the cockpit and loudly proclaimed, "Hi, pilots! My name's Gwennie! But really my name's Gwendolyn!"

Our hearts melted, putty in her charming little hands.

...And then a little passenger's innocent joy breaks the somber mood...

And then it hit me. That little girl. So full of joy. Of innocence. Of life. That's why our hero had sacrificed his.

And it was not in vain.

"To fly West, my friend, is a flight we must all take for a final check."
—Author Unknown

I did not have the honor of serving my country, but I would like to personally thank the military veterans in my family: my father Richard (Navy Petty Officer on a Destroyer during WWII), brother Allen (Vietnam M-60-toting infantry grunt) and nephew Daniel (Gulf War I Marine.)

Airman Owens and wife Brianna.

Dedicated to the memory of Sr. Airman Dustin Howard Owens, lost to us March 19, 2014 while serving his country in Osan Air Base, Republic of Korea. Owen is survived by his wife Brianna and children AmyLynn, Mavvrick, EllyMae and expected daughter TessieAnn (born after his loss on May 23, 2014.)

3 yo Dustin receives his daddy's flag. Like his father, proud to hold and serve the symbol of his country. Photo courtesy Stacey Kay Photography.

SECTION 8: Novel Idea! Book Excerpts

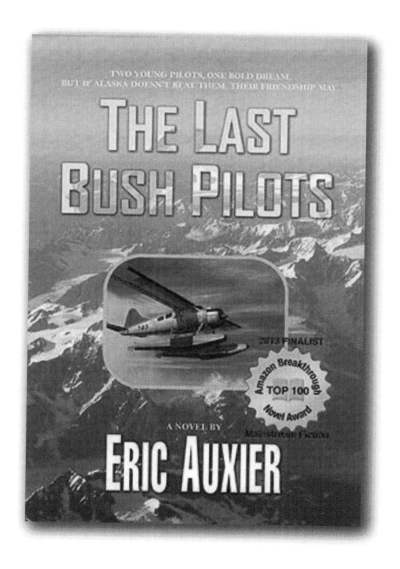

THE LAST BUSH PILOTS

"You won't want to put it down while the midnight sun still shines!"—Airways Magazine

Two young pilots. One bold dream.
But if Alaska doesn't beat them, their friendship may.

"TOP 100, Mainstream Fiction"
Amazon 2013 Breakthrough Novel Awards

PRAISE FOR **THE LAST BUSH PILOTS**

"Eric Auxier is the next Tom Clancy of aviation."
—Tawni Waters, ***Beauty of the Broken; Siren Song; Top Travel Writers of 2010***

"I flew through ***The Last Bush Pilots*** in one sitting, keeping my seatbelt securely fastened. A fast-paced tale, thoroughly enjoyed."
—John Wegg, Editor *Airways* Magazine

"The author paints pictures with words that are every bit as beautiful and moving as anything ever drawn or photographed."
—aviationguy.com

"A page-turning adventure novel, where surviving is only half the battle."
—Mark L. Berry, airline pilot-author, ***13,760 Feet: My Personal Hole in the Sky***

"Captain Auxier takes you into another world—one that he has lived. The place were pilots are born, and many have died."
—Karlene Petitt, airline pilot-author, ***Flight for Safety;*** and ***Flight for Control***

"With 12,000+ hours of arctic Alaskan bush flying , reading ***The Last Bush Pilots*** was like a glance in a forty year old mirror. Nice work, Eric."
—CloudDancer, author, ***"CloudDancer's Alaskan Chronicles."***

Book Trailer: vimeo.com/capnaux/lbp

Excerpt:
A Crash in the Wilderness

"Mayday, mayday, I'm going down!"

The frantic radio call rang in DC Alva's earphones. Instantly he recognized the pilot's voice: his best friend Allen Foley.

"Engine failure, south of Davidson Glacier," Allen's transmission continued. Then fell silent.

DC's guts churned. The glacier, the young pilot knew, was miles from civilization—and help. Worse, flying visually beneath the clouds as all Alaska bush pilots did, Allen would have mere seconds to save the plane.

Shoving the throttle full forward, DC banked his floatplane hard left, north up the coastline toward the crash site. The engine surged. The manifold pressure needle straddled red line. He crowded the rugged slopes of the Chilkat Range. Pine trees dense as shag carpet loomed below.

Taku winds tumbled like whitewater over the cliffs and pummeled his craft. Left hand gripped tight about the control yoke and right hand working the throttle, he fought to keep the aircraft upright.

With trembling voice, DC relayed the distress call to headquarters. "SEAS Base, this is *Sitka Shrike*," he radioed, using the company's designated call sign for his plane. "*Gastineau King* just called, 'Mayday.' Engine's failed. South of Davidson. I'm enroute now."

Another crash, DC thought. One was seven times more likely to be struck by lightning, for God's sake. But once again, lightning had struck too close. The question burning in the back of his mind always was, Who next? Only in his darkest nightmares had he imagined . . .

Allen would be down by now. Images flashed through DC's mind of the man dying beneath a smoldering wreck. Instinctively he shoved again on the throttle, already firewalled.

"*Shrike* to *King*, do you read?" DC called. No reply. "*King*, this is *Shrike*, come in!" Static.

DC leaned over the controls and squinted through the plexiglass. Drizzle cut his view up the channel to a myopic three miles. Each visual cue, each bulge in the land or curve in the shore, floated toward him through the misty curtain like ghosts in a fog-shrouded graveyard.

"Coastline. Got to keep the coastline in sight," DC mumbled, not realizing he'd voiced the thought aloud. The leaden sky pressed down on him like the slab roof of a tomb. And it might as well be made of cement, he thought: fly into it, or penetrate the blinding rain ahead, and splat across the first mountain that came along. The moist air pressed through the cabin's filters and cooled his cheeks. He shivered, more from fear than chill. The drizzle turned to rain and formed a wall around him. The drops pelted his windshield. With each moment, the terrain popped through the curtain ever closer—visibility dropping fast. Less than a mile, he figured.

"Damnit," he cursed, throttling back. For Allen, every minute lost was a mile closer to death. But in this weather, speed was DC's first enemy. Any worse, and he would have to turn back or land.

The De Havilland Beaver floatplane slowed. As the airspeed trickled down, DC lowered a section of flaps to compensate. The trailing edge of the wings extended downward, adding lift.

He eyed the waves near shore. Chop the size of Volkswagens.

DC grimaced. Even landing *with* engine power, he could dig a float or catch a wing and flip.

Allen, flying a fixed-gear wheel plane, had even less hope. High tide covered the soft beach. Ocean waves slammed against a rocky shoreline, backed by a forest wall. Nowhere could he have glided to safety.

"*Shrike* to *King*, do you read?" DC called, for the hundredth time it seemed. "*King*, come in. At least key the mike, Damnit." No reply. "SEAS Base, what about rescue?"

"Coast Guard chopper's launched from Sitka, ETA one hour," the dispatcher's voice crackled.

"Can you make it through?" another pilot asked.

He eyed the wall of water ahead. "I—I'm not sure."

"Negative, *Shrike*," his Chief Pilot's voice cut in. "Weather's too solid. Seas are too rough for you, DC. Turn back."

But he couldn't shake the image of the dying man from his mind. He pressed on, squeezed between cloud and ground.

An hour passed—or a minute, he couldn't tell.

The drenched air formed fog; all turned murky. Forest, beach, even the air itself retreated into shadows of twilight. The saturated atmosphere phased between the elements of cloud and sky, water and air.

"Holy—" his voice trailed off. His gut churned. He'd heard of the phenomenon but had never seen it; never believed it could happen.

The sky fell.

The cloud base dropped, sucking the air below into its fold.

DC pushed forward on the yoke. The plane dove. He led the plummeting ceiling by a mere wingspan. The altimeter needle spun through five hundred feet.

Below the legal limit, he thought. But FAA rules were the least of his worries.

Four hundred . . three hundred . . the needle spiraled downward.

A glance out the side window: treetops whizzed by, inches below his floats. A startled eagle took wing.

"*Shrike*, I say again. Turn back immediately," his Chief Pilot ordered. *But his life's in my hands*, he thought.

His hands. He looked at them, tight and trembling about the controls.

Flying through this weather was hazardous at best.

Flying through this weather could mean two accidents.

Flying through this weather would take all the training and all the experience he'd strived to gain while flying the Alaska bush—which, he realized now, was pitifully little.

If he crashed, his dream of flying for the airlines would crash too.

If he survived.

DC swallowed hard.

And made the toughest decision of his life.

CODE NAME: DODGER

**Winner, Young Adult Category
Remington Literary's Search for a Best First Novel**

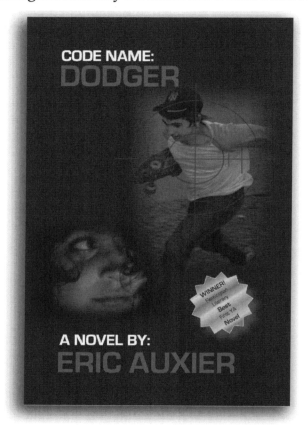

*Rebellious teen orphan Justin Reed and beautiful illegal immigrant
Mira must outwit Justin's father's killer—the evil enemy spy Pharaoh.*

PRAISE FOR **CODE NAME: DODGER**

"An all-time fun ride! The author hit a big win on this. Looking forward to the series!"—Karlene Petitt, airline pilot-author, *Flight for Safety*; and *Flight for Control*

"Like *Harry Potter*, this YA novel is fun for kids of all ages. While ostensibly a spy thriller, full of twists and turns, high tech spy gadgets, ruses and deceptions, *Code Name: Dodger* goes far deeper, into conflicted characters, their complex relationships, and the true meaning of love, loyalty and family."—Tawni Waters, author, *Beauty of the Broken; Siren Song; Top Travel Writers of 2010*

"I'm 50 years older than the target market, and I couldn't put the book down! The story line is extremely well crafted, and the first person narrative puts the reader into the protagonist's shoes. If you have a teenager who doesn't like to read, hand him this book and he'll be hooked!" —George Nolly

Book Trailer: <u>*vimeo.com/capnaux/cnd*</u>

Excerpt from Code Name: Dodger

TOP SECRET
EYES ONLY

TO: KING COLE/CIA HQ
FR: AGENT FAGIN
LOC: NORTH BROOKLYN, NY
RE: ENEMY AGENT PHARAOH
OP: RUBBER SOUL

HAVE DISCOVERED CIA ENEMY AGENT PHARAOH'S PRIMARY TARGET: REED, JUSTIN M.; TEEN ORPHAN; SON OF MALCOMB REED, DECEASED. ENEMY AGENT OBJCTV: & IDENT: UNKN.
　　END MSG.

　　I sat beside my parents' graves all afternoon, all evening, the sun setting, darkness falling. Beams from the half moon pierced the foliage and broke my trance.

　　Sitting back, I surveyed their final resting place. With these two mounds, I buried my two pasts. I brushed the dirt from my palms and stood.

　　"I'll join you someday, Mom and Dad. But it won't be soon."

　　"Sooner than you think, Justin."

　　I jumped and turned in surprise. I spied a man lurking in the shadows of an elm. I couldn't see his face, but his raspy voice I knew too well.

"Pharaoh!"

I thought I'd shouted his name, but all that came from me was a whisper. Out of the shadows, he stepped toward me.

Then I saw his face, disfigured from the explosion. I gasped in horror. His left eye was swollen shut in blue black, pussed and wrinkled skin. A scar creased his left cheek and pulled his lips down into a lopsided frown. His left hand, injured from a bullet, hung in a sling. Then I saw the Glock pistol leveled at me from his right hand.

I froze, unable to move, to think, to breathe.

"How did you—"

"Survive? Didn't you ever read about trap doors and secret passageways in your little spy books, boy?" He limped forward. "Or do you mean, how did I find you? Quite simple really, where else would you go? Typical, stupid little teen."

He edged closer. I glanced right and left, looking for a place to run, to hide.

"Oh, no, Artful Dodger, you can't dodge me now. And no one's around to hear your screams. But don't worry. I'm going to give you what you dearly want most. I'm going to send you to see your parents."

"N-no." I backed away. I bumped into Mom's headstone.

"*Chiyaa!*" A roundhouse kick struck my face and knocked me backward over the grave marker.

The kick stunned me, but training took over. I somersaulted backward and stood. Another blow sent me tumbling to the ground. I don't know whether it had been from a fist or a foot, but it bloodied my nose.

I lay on my hands and knees, unable to escape. I closed my lips tight and breathed through my nostrils like a winded horse.

He grabbed the back of my belt, lifted, and threw me head first into Dad's gravestone. Streaks of light darted about my eyes. I fell to the ground, panting. Dirt and blood mixed on my tongue and filled my nostrils. I choked and coughed. Grit crunched between my teeth.

I heard two quick clicks, the unique sound of a silencer locking into place.

I craned my stiff neck around. My left eye was swollen shut, like his. My whole sight was bathed in red, from the blood vessels swelled up inside my eyeball. His blurry figure towered over me, lit in small patches of moonbeam. His one eye, open wide in rage, stared down, round and aglow like a second moon. He cocked the pistol and leveled it at me. His uneven frown twisted into an insane grimace.

I rolled onto my back.

He raised the pistol high above his head, then, ever so slowly, lowered it down, down to take careful aim at my skull.

My muscles went limp.

I closed my eyes.

CODE NAME: DODGER, MISSION 2
CARTEL KIDNAPPING
COMING SOON!

TOP SECRET—EYES ONLY—FLASH TRAFFIC
TO: KING COLE/CIA HQ
FM: AGENT ANACONDA/IXTAPA, MEXICO
RE: OPERATION SNAKE BITE
DISCOVERED MEX. DRUG LORD CARLOS OCHO HAS DISPATCHED TOP ASSASSINS TO U.S. SUSPECT RETALIATION AGAINST AGENTS FAGIN AND DODGER FOR DESTROYING THE OCHO/PHARAOH SMUGGLING RING. URGENT ACTION REQUIRED TO ENSURE THEIR SAFETY.
END MSG.

"No more trouble, or I shoot you both," Pablo warned, jabbing a finger at us.. He sat us down on a log in the middle of our fishing camp, deep in the woods and far from help. A henchman held an uzi machine gun to our backs. Pablo reached into his satchel and pulled out a walkie-talkie. He held it to his lips and spoke, turning from us as he did. He announced in Spanish, "Conquistador, this is Fisherman. We have Agent Fagin and his boy. Proceed inbound for extraction. These GPS coordinates."

I looked questioningly at Bob. With his eyes he motioned to his lap, directing my attention to his bound hands. One covered the other so that only I could see his fingers. Slowly, silently, he "spoke" in deaf sign language, forming letters with his fingers. I had learned some basic sign during CIA communications training, so I easily read his message: "Pharaoh's Mexican contacts," he spelled.

I tensed at the mention of Pharaoh. "Smugglers?" I asked with my hands. He nodded.

"What do they want?" I signed back.

"Revenge." A chill zapped down my spine.

Pablo turned and faced us. Playing with his huge knife, Pablo slowly circled us. Each time he went behind, it was all I could do to keep breathing. At any moment, I expected the blade to be thrust through my back.

Finally, Pablo crouched down before Bob. Slowly, menacingly, he played the buck knife across Bob's cheeks, as if giving him a shave.

"So tell me, Agent *Fagin*," he began, using Bob's top secret CIA code name. "Who is this great *Agent Dodger*?"

I bit my tongue, trying my best not to react. Bob stiffened, and tightened his lips.

"Tell me now, and we save much time. You die fast, no pain. I might even let de little boy go free. Minus a finger for a souvenir, heh heh." He slid the knife up and down Bob's throat. Bob flinched as the knife bit into his skin, drawing a trickle of blood. "I know he must be *biiig* boss man to bring down the great spy Pharaoh. So big, there is no CIA record. He not even exist. So I know. He big, big boss man. So I ask: who is the great Artful Dodger? And what does he know about the Ocho organization, hmm?" Bob stared straight ahead in defiance.

I wondered what Pablo would do if Bob told him the truth, that "the great Agent Artful Dodger" was sitting right next to him. A scrawny little orphan kid with hardly two cents to his name. Probably laugh his head off. Then take ours.

A new sound floated in on the breeze. I looked west through the pine tops and down the canyon, and could just make out a speck in the sky. The *whop-whop* grew louder and echoed through the canyon. Sunlight flashed off the rotors as the speck formed into the shape of a helicopter. I wished for a U.S. Forest Service chopper or, better yet, a CIA bird. But that was hopeless.

I shut my eyes against the blast of dust as the chopper circled overhead, sizing up the landing area. He finally decided to come up the river and through a cut in the trees next to camp. The craft settled onto the bed of soft earth, green ferns and dry pine needles in front of us.

"Get in." Luis barked, prodding us onto the six seat chopper and boarding behind us. I sat in the far corner from the door, facing rearward, with Bob next to me. Pablo took an empty seat facing us. Luis slammed the door shut and threw himself in the seat opposite me. Enraged, his eyes burned into mine. I lowered my head, and sobered up to the desperate situation Bob and I were in.

Revenge, I thought to myself. They—*he*—wants revenge.

A guard squeezed in and sat by the door, next to Bob. By the guy's wide eyes and tense muscles, I could tell he'd never been in a helicopter before. Neither had I, but I'd flown a lot. The guard leveled a shaky pistol at us and clutched the arm rest with his other hand.

The whine of the turbine engines increased and the rotor blades began to whirl at blinding speed. My guts sank as the helicopter lifted.

The guard stiffened and whimpered, clutching tighter at the arm rest. He stared longingly out the window in the door. I traded glances with Bob; he'd noticed the guard's distraction too.

If there was just some way to break free, and hide from the goons on the ground . . . .

Any escape had to come now. Right now.

The pilot gingerly floated the craft between the trees and out over the rushing river. We inched along downstream toward the pool next to camp. Only ten feet above the water, I figured. If we could just jump out and hide somewhere. I had an idea.

I coughed loudly to get Bob's attention, then nodded to my lap. My hands were still bound at the wrists, so I covered one hand with the other and slowly signed the word, "R-I-V-E-R." I ended by pointing a thumb out the window. Instantly my adopted father/CIA trainer caught my meaning. He signaled back a countdown by slowly retracting each finger on one hand: 5-4-3-2-1.

Bob exploded into action. He elbowed the guard in the chin then launched his entire body at Luis and Pablo. I lunged for the door and popped it open. Screaming, the guard recoiled, powerless to stop me in his panic. I jumped halfway out, but someone caught my legs. I twisted around to see Luis snarling back, his hands an iron grip on my legs.

I hung out of the chopper at the knees, my back to the earth like an astronaut in a space capsule. I writhed at Luis' hold, but couldn't break free.

"Help me Georgio!" Luis shouted to the terrified guard. The man hesitated, then aimed an unsteady pistol at me. Luis turned back and yelled, "Reed, get in here or Georgio shoots you."

The helicopter lurched as Bob knocked Pablo into the pilot. Georgio dropped his gun and, screaming, grabbed for the arm rest. The pistol clattered out of the cabin. I grabbed wildly for it but missed. The weapon sailed out and splashed into the waters far below.

The pilot fought to regain control as the two foes battled in his cockpit. The chopper rocked and spun over the water, hovering dangerously close to the trees. The pilot edged the ship toward an opening to lift out of the foliage. The chance to escape was quickly fading.

We cleared the trees and the pilot gunned the throttle. We shot skyward. The g-force snapped me down against the hull, and the back of my head bashed the landing skid. For a dazed moment I stared, upside down, at the river dropping away. I blinked and shook off the vertigo, then turned back to Luis. He struggled to pull me in, but the extra weight of the g-force was too much for him.

He shouted, "Georgio, you *estupido*, snap out of it and help me or I'll shoot you myself! Grab his other leg," he commanded. The guard reluctantly knelt on the floor and grabbed my ankle. The two dragged me in.

The helicopter rocked suddenly as Bob and Pablo fell struggling into the cockpit. The ship dropped, and for a moment I felt weightless. I used the motion to reach up and grab Georgio's collar.

The pilot recovered and gunned it again, and earth dropped away.

"*Adios*, Georgio!" I yelled, then yanked hard at his collar. I kicked up into his stomach and flipped him over my head and out of the chopper.

"*Ahh!*" he screamed as he dropped away. That left one leg free.

"Sayonara, *estupido*!" I shouted at Luis. Then stomped on his hawk nose with my heel.

"*Aghh!*" he cried, falling back into the cabin and letting go of my leg. I realized, too late, that I was still more out of the helicopter than in.

It seemed like I plummeted forever, like in a dream. Adrenaline rushed through me like the river rapids. Time slowed. The chopper's rotor blades seemed to turn in slow motion—*whop! . . . whop! . . . whop!*.

I flapped my arms like the blades, trying desperately to spin around and at least hit whatever was below feet first. One, two, three, four . . . twelve rotations of the rotor blades.

Impact.

AFTERWARD

Photo courtesy michaelhesley.blogspot.com

Ladies and gentlemen, from the flight deck, this is your Cap'n speaking. I hope you've enjoyed our flight! I have good news and bad news for you.

The bad: for now, we've reached the end of our journey!

The good news: work on Volume II is already in progress!

In the meantime, feel free to visit me over on capnaux.com, and drop me a line any time at capnaux@gmail.com.

More links to my stuff, such as Twitter, Facebook, etc. are listed in the next section.

This is Cap'n Aux . . . signing off!

LINKS to All Things Cap'n Aux

"Airline pilot by day, writer by night, kid by choice."
—Cap'n Aux

AUTHOR'S BLOG

Adventures of Cap'n Aux: capnaux.com

The Last Bush Pilots & other works

Amazon Author Page: amazon.com/author/ericauxier

To explore more about *The Last Bush Pilots*: lastbushpilots.com

To order in Print: www.createspace.com/4053153

To order in eBook: goo.gl/NCvGuW

To order on iTunes: ibookstore.com/products.php?i=1480279889

Book Trailer: vimeo.com/52958425

Mayday! Trailer: vimeo.com/capnaux/mayday

Code Name: Dodger Trailer: vimeo.com/capnaux/cnd

To explore more about *Code name: Dodger*: capnaux.com/code-name-dodger/

Cap'n Aux swag from Cafe Press! www.cafepress.com/CapnAuxSwag

Social Media

Facebook: www.facebook.com/CapnAux

Twitter: twitter.com/capnaux

Instagram: instagram.com/capnaux

Google +: plus.google.com/+EricAuxiercapnaux/posts

Vimeo Page: vimeo.com/capnaux

Livin' the Dream! Featured Video: vimeo.com/capnaux/livinthedream

Stories on NYCAviation.com: www.nycaviation.com/author/eauxier/

Cap'n Aux Aviation App (Beta): appstore.monk.ee/details.php?
appid=100154756

Contact the Author

Email: capnaux@gmail.com

About the end-of-story marker

This is a photo of me landing at KFLL, courtesy of Mark Lawrence of amateuravphoto.blogspot.com. He also took the shot that graces the cover of this book. Check Mark's bio out on the "About the Cover" page!

ABOUT THE AUTHOR

Eric "Cap'n Aux" Auxier is a pilot by day, writer by night, and kid by choice.

Never one to believe in working for a living, his past list of occupations include: Alaska bush pilot, freelance writer, mural artist, and pilot for a Caribbean seaplane operation. He is now a captain for a major U.S. airline.

Mr. Auxier has contributed to such worldwide publications as *Arizona Highways*, *Airways* Magazine, *Plane & Pilot* and *AOPA Pilot*. He is a graduate of Arizona State University (B.S. degree in Aeronautical Technology; minors in Journalism and Japanese) and Cochise College (A.S. degree in Pro-Pilot and Creative Writing). At both institutions, he worked as a newspaper editor, staff reporter and columnist. He is currently a columnist for NYCAviation.com and a regular contributor to *Airways* Magazine.

There I Wuz! is his third book. His second, **The Last Bush Pilots**, a novel inspired by his adventures as a young bush pilot in Alaska, captured the coveted **Amazon 2013 Top 100 Breakthrough Novels Award**. The award-winning *Code Name: Dodger* is his first novel, a young adult spy adventure.

He is currently working on two new works, ***There I Wuz! Volume II***, and ***Cartel Kidnapping***, Book Two of the ***Code Name: Dodger*** adventure series.

A portion of all proceeds from Mr. Auxier's works go to the international orphan relief funds, Warmblankets.org and flyingkites.org.

Mr. Auxier makes his home in Phoenix, Arizona.

ABOUT THE COVER

COVER PHOTO—MARK LAWRENCE

Photographer Mark Lawrence is an avgeek that has been around the industry since he was a small child. An aviation photographer for many years, he is also the Producer for the aviation website <u>NYCAviation.com</u>. He makes his home in Fort Lauderdale, Florida with his wife and son. email: mark@tavustheman.com.

blog: <u>amateuravphoto.blogspot.com</u> portfolio: <u>marklawrence.zenfolio.com</u>

COVER DESIGN—GINO LUIS AVENTURERA

Gino Luis Aventurera is an artist and graphic designer. He also collaborated with Eric Auxier on the cover of the novel, **The Last Bush Pilots**. He is a graduate student from Arizona State University and is currently residing in Mesa, Arizona.

email: ginoluis@hotmail.com

COMING SOON: VOLUME 2!

MORE...

—Adventures   —Inflight Emergencies   —Tough Lessons
—Stories behind the stories   —Love, Laughs and Tears in the Sky
—Guest Stories   —Gone with the Hurricane, Part 2

PLUS...

—New Photo Section (ebook version)!   —New Q&A Section!
—New surprises!

KEEP AN EYE ON THE SKIES: COMING SOON!

Made in the USA
San Bernardino, CA
26 July 2014